T0299456

How to
Drink Wine

How to
Drink Wine

Tom Surgey

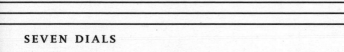

SEVEN DIALS

First published in Great Britain in 2024 by Seven Dials,
an imprint of The Orion Publishing Group Ltd
Carmelite House, 50 Victoria Embankment
London EC4Y 0DZ

An Hachette UK Company

10 9 8 7 6 5 4 3 2 1

A CIP catalogue record for this book is
available from the British Library.

ISBN (Hardback) 978 1 399615181
ISBN (eBook) 978 1 399615198
ISBN (Audio) 978 1 399615204

Designed by Helen Ewing
Printed in Great Britain by Clays Ltd, Elcograf S.p.A

MIX
Paper | Supporting
responsible forestry
FSC
www.fsc.org
FSC® C104740

www.orionbooks.co.uk

Dedicated to 'the girls'

Olivia Surgey – partner in everything. Cheerleader.
Reality checker. Inspiration. Best friend. Without whom
I would have drifted off-course more often and far too far.
In fact, I wouldn't even be on a course. I will be grateful forever.
I love you beyond words.

Beatrix and Flora Surgey – Everything. Always. Outrageous.
Pure joy. Unimaginable love.

Contents

Foreword:
Tom's Take on Wine

I'm not a geek. I'm not a collector. I'm not a critic. I'm an enjoyer. I hope I can inspire you to be the same. It's the best and, I feel, the most authentic approach to this ridiculously lovely stuff called wine.

That said, I've amassed a fair amount of knowledge about wine over the years, both through formal study and, more importantly, from well over a decade of total commitment to 'getting stuck in' with a voracity and passion that, I'm led to believe, is both unusual and, at times, life-threatening. It's my career and my hobby. In so many ways, it is my life.

Without realising it at the time, this book has been two decades in the making. It was only a year in the writing, though, and I enjoyed every minute of it. My journey into wine, from working in the pubs, bars and restaurants of Sussex, Suffolk and London since the age of fourteen, has given me a relatively practical and pragmatic approach to it. And I didn't inherit a love or knowledge of wine. Quite the opposite. It wasn't on my radar at all. I found beer first, then whisky. Wine found me in miniscule sample after miniscule sample on busy dining-room floors. It found me in the dregs of iconic bottles left after service by generous diners keen to share their experience. We shared them as a team in suddenly silent dining rooms at 1a.m., with a Heineken in the other hand. Then we went to Café Boheme and drank pitchers of lager and smoky Laphroaig chasers until the sun came up over Soho.

Those outrageous nights are largely behind me. I'm pretty sensible now. I am a genuine and true devotee of the 'drink less, drink better' mantra. Apart from the occasional blip, when I find myself away from parental responsibility and get a little over excited. Alcohol, at its best, is a phenomenal social lubricant; a catalyst for building communities, relationships, whole cultures. Fermentation preserves the natural flavours of grapes grown in a specific location. Wine is, therefore, a transportive drink, a window to a specific place and time, both the natural elements and the human culture, preserved like a bug in amber.

The future of alcohol in an increasingly health-conscious modern society depends on us getting to grips with alcohol as an elevator of already-great experiences. It is a drink that brings us closer to people and places in every corner of the world. The focus should be on having a quality experience. That's where we're all heading sooner or later.

The snag here is that the vast majority of us find the idea of wine overwhelming. There is a pervading sense that good wine is an intellectual pursuit for the initiated few. We feel anxiety about picking the 'wrong' wine. Beer doesn't have this issue. We enjoy the exploration of new beers. We may or may not remember the name of the brewer. We probably don't even try. We're there for pure enjoyment, not concerned with cataloguing the details.

I need you to get to this place with wine, too. Being in the moment. Enjoying the experience. Embracing the complexity. Leaving your imposter syndrome at the door. To do this, a little knowledge helps. That's where this book comes in; it's the useful stuff I have learnt while working and playing in wine. A modern, practical 101 guide to get you feeling comfy and enjoying wine with the pure-joy and abandon both you and it deserve.

This book is my attempt to articulate the learnings, both factual and emotional, I've gained over the years. I want it to be genuinely beneficial to help you get 'into' wine. I want you to become comfortable, to feel as if you have every reason and right to drink wine and swirl it about aloofly in any company you care to keep. Be louche. Be loose.

What it isn't is an exhaustive list of facts to prepare you for a wine exam. There are many great, highly geeky wine books with specialisms on specific regions, winemaking, the works. I love them. You will, too. Let this be your gateway into those, but this is not that.

This book will set you up with a thorough understanding of the core principles that make wine 'wine'. It is everything you need to know to enjoy the drinking of it and enjoy making conscious choices about it. It will give you the grounding to hold your own when 'wine chat' erupts. Stepping into a wine shop or being handed the wine list will become an opportunity, not a challenge. You will have the framework of understanding, appreciation of the nuances, and know the right questions to ask to get the best from every wine-drinking scenario.

I hope it lights a fire for you, igniting an enthusiastic and emotionally connected relationship with the good stuff that lasts a lifetime. You can't win wine. No one's right or wrong about it. There are very few ways to fuck this up, really. So, stay loose, Pickle.

On that note, let's get into it. It starts with a relatively chunky paragraph or two about yeast. It was a surprise to me, too, to be honest. Bear with me – we're making good headway now.

1.

The Key Principles, According to Tom

Fermentation is Everywhere

Fermentation, of one kind or another, is everywhere. It's worth knowing a bit about. In fact, we consume minute quantities of alcohol regularly as we graze about our daily lives. A wide variety of yeasts exist naturally in every conceivable environment between -2°C and 45°C, from your gut, to your home, to deep below the sea. In anaerobic environments, when these millennia-old, single-cell members of the fungus family encounter sugar, they get stuck in like it's a wedding. The result is alcoholic fermentation. As you read this, yeasts are staging a raid on the sugars in your fruit bowl and they've had their way with that loaf in the bread bin. Anything with yeast and sugar present has the potential to ferment. The natural process of fermentation only really stops when either the yeast becomes inactive, the sugar runs out or MC Hammer insists.

However, there's no alcohol in your cheese, yoghurt or chorizo. While these are fermented, it's bacteria rather than yeast causing the fermentation, and that doesn't produce booze. Sometimes, there are bacteria present in an alcoholic fermentation to add complexity, but they consume the alcohol as it's produced; this is how you make low- or no-alcohol fermented kombucha. It's hugely complex. The key thing to remember is that fermentations are everywhere; they're all great but we're focussing on the alcoholic ones.

In these alcoholic fermentations, yeasts convert sugars into a range of metabolic by-products. These (if it's nice, say it twice) metabolic by-products are mainly ethanol (alcohol) and carbon dioxide, which are key components of wine and, your friend and mine, fizzy wine.

In a world of widespread little fermentations, the poetry-inspiring, millennia-old, cultural cornerstone that is wine is really just the creative peak of a ubiquitous natural activity.

Winemakers are simply custodians of their specific fermentation. They endeavour to control this natural process to a greater or lesser extent, steering it, or being steered by it, towards a conclusion that fits their, or the wine's, ambitions.

While we talk fermentation, I reckon wine has a solid shout for being the greatest of fermented beverages. Even when you consider great beers, the base alcohols that make the finest spirits, or anything else that might have a rightful claim to being very special, wine provides the most transparent and pure window to its place of origin. Most drinks are made using complex recipes, relying on multiple added components, like hops, and undergo processes, such as malting of starches or adding water to stretch them out. In its simplest form, however, wine is just grapes – squished, fermented with yeasts and bottled. Fermentation preserves the grapes' unique character, holding every nuance together in tantalisingly explorable, harmonious layers.

The complexities and potential pathways that fermentation can follow make for diverse textures and flavours developing in the wine. There are many different yeasts and each gives a distinct character to the finished wine. Some are specifically selected and added as a culture, while others may be naturally present in and around the winery. Some stay the duration, having a large impact on the wine, others die out early on in the fermentation process or are blocked by the winemaker. It isn't just ethanol and carbon dioxide that are the outcomes – new acid structures, multiple types of minor alcohols and a spider web of potential interactions between these newly created compounds have profound and notable effects on the final wine, be it to make it richer, fuller, more crisp, fruitier or more restrained.

I am being outrageously blasé in my over-simplification of fermentation here. This is as much as you need to know to appreciate and enjoy wine, but it may not be quite sufficient to bore your dinner guests fully or cause your other half to bury their head under the sofa cushions. So, feel free to delve deeper into the world of fermentation if these are your objectives. Or just because it is endlessly fascinating.

It's All About Grapes

So, fermentation contributes the alcohol and layers of possible textures and flavours derived by acids and alcohols endlessly twiddling about with each other. That's all well and good, but it would be for nought without the core flavours of delicious fruits, zippy acidity and cheek-pinching tannin that makes wine 'wine'. For these we need grapes. And it's grapes alone, I'm afraid; no blueberry wine here. Grapes offer a rare combination of high-sugar development (enough to produce good quantities of alcohol without needing the addition of extra sugar) and retained fresh acidity. They also give scope for a huge variety of flavours and aromas in the finished wine. Other fruits, by comparison, give one-dimensional, comparatively 'boring' results. Millenia ago, humans decided grapes made the best wine and we're of the same mindset today. The earliest evidence of humans intentionally domesticating wild vines and cultivating them for wine production appears about 8,000 years ago (6,000 BC) in an area between the mountains of east Turkey, and Georgia and Armenia's Caucasus Mountains. The wild vines (*vitis vinifera*) propagated by these peoples, and each winemaking culture across the world since, gave favour to plants that achieved higher-sugar, more aromatic, flavourful grapes. As cultures and eventually empires (see the Greeks, Romans, etc.) embraced wine, they transported the culture (and the vines) with them as they went. Domesticated *vitis vinifera* cuttings spread across Europe and the East, and eventually the Americas. These cultivated vines joined the indigenous, wild vines in the environments where they arrived, sometimes cross fertilising naturally and sometimes by human hand, further widening the diversity of varieties being used to make wine.

Fun fact: almost all winemaking grape vines are hermaphroditic; meaning they have both male and female anatomy and self-pollinate. No birds or bees required. Not all wild vines are hermaphroditic, though. In fact, it's rare for them to be so. Most are either male or female, requiring interaction to pollinate. It is the selection, over millennia, by humans of hermaphroditic variants of wild vines, for ease and consistency of produce year-on-year, that has resulted in the winemaking vines getting it done by themselves. It also saves endless swiping through Tinder and awkward first dates.

In nature's family tree, vines encompass an enormous number of climbing plants and creepers. All lovely, if a bit grabby, but we're solely focussed on the genus *vitis* here. *Vitis* embraces all grape-producing vines and includes many dozens of vine species. Of these species only six or so are used to produce wine and one reigns supreme – *vitis vinifera*, the European grape vine. Between *vitis vinifera* and its lesser-used but still important American relatives (*vitis labrusca* for example), there are around 10,000 vine varieties, each capable of producing a wine distinct from another. In commercial cultivation today, we make wine with a mere 1,500 of these, with only a few dozen famous varieties getting most of the limelight and taking up the majority of plantings.

The diversity doesn't stop there, I'm afraid. Each grape variety, for example Pinot Noir, has dozens (sometimes more!) of variants, each with its own slight nuances and individual attributes; perhaps larger berries, thicker or thinner skins, a more or less aromatic character, etc. Sometimes this is caused by natural mutations but, more often than not, it's caused by humans selecting the most successful individual vines in a vineyard to be the specimen from which future vineyards are propagated. As vines are transported to new climates and soils, or as winemakers wish for different attributes to be more prominent in their wines, this selection process eventually forms a new variant of the original perfectly suited to its new environment. In turn, this successful variant becomes dominant in that area and its subtle nuances become synonymous with the wines of that region. These isolated variants are known as 'clones', and winemakers now have many different clones to choose from when planting new vineyards for any given grape variety.

Each grape variety has its own particular preferences in terms of temperature, rain levels, soil types, etc., and so is best suited to its own particular part of the world. Grapevines that have not travelled but, instead, have evolved where they originated have adapted to suit their regions perfectly. Known as indigenous varietals, these are less famous, since they haven't been picked up and planted the world over, and they represent some of the most exciting, off-the-beaten-track wines you can experience today. Portugal and Italy are key treasure troves for these, but are by no means the only countries with exciting indigenous varietals.

That said, the big-name international varieties, like Chardonnay, originated somewhere in particular, too, despite being planted in almost every winemaking region of the world today. It's around Burgundy in central France for Chard, as it happens . . .

Acidity

From the vines, to the fruit. The grapes have got a whole bunch of stuff going on inside them. Wine makes use of almost all their available elements. As grapes grow on the vine, photosynthesis (one for all you GCSE biology nostalgists) creates sugars from sunlight, water and carbon dioxide. Essentially, the more sunshine, the more sugar is created and the riper the grapes become. As this takes place, the natural acidity in the grapes is changing, too. Malic acid (a super-tart, cooking-apple-style acid with a sharp edge) is the dominant acid when the grape is unripe. As it ripens, malic acids reduce and a new acid – tartaric – builds to become the dominant one. Tartaric acid is slightly less sharp than malic. The warmer the climate, the higher the tartaric acid content and the lower the malic acid content. In very cool climates (like the UK), malic and tartaric acids can be quite close in quantity, making the resulting wines very tart. Whatever the ratio, tartaric is always the main acid in ripe grapes.

As the ripening grape swells with sugar and water, however, the ratio of these acids to sugars reduces and the grape gets sweeter. In cooler, less sunny climates, photosynthesis happens more slowly and the grapes ultimately reach lower ripeness levels than in a hot climate. As a result, the acids remain higher proportionally and the sugars lower. Fermentation converts the available sugars to alcohol, so lower sugars equal lower levels of alcohol, resulting in zingy, fresh, mouthwatering wines. In a hot, sunny climate, the opposite happens – sugars rise quickly, acids drop faster and grapes become very sweet. The resulting wines can be juicy and delicious, but may also be overly alcoholic and a bit flabby without enough refreshing acid. These poles of cool and hot are the two extremes; with every possible climate in between. Generally speaking, cooler climates make lighter wines with a finer structure, warmer climates make richer, fuller wines and medium to warm climates achieve a balance.

Alongside the sugar and acid development, the ripening grapes build flavour and take on colour. There is an outrageously wide array of unique aromatic characters and flavour compounds in grapes, each contributing little and large qualities to the finished wine. These different flavour compounds are present in differing quantities depending on grape varietal, location and weather; giving us the enormous diversity of styles of wine available.

Colour

Whether white, black or gris, somewhere in between, the colour of the grapes' skin develops as they ripen. After flowering, the vine's fruit appears first as bright green, sparse little bunches of tiny, hard grapes. As they ripen, the varieties with darker skins take on a deeper hue, while those with lighter skins become more translucent and pale. The longer, warmer and sunnier the ripening period before harvest, the more colour builds in the grapes.

Talking about a wine's colour gives you enormous opportunity to use a very 'winey' word indeed. It's up there in the top tier of wine-geeky phrases. I implore you to know it, store it away and (crucially) never use it in polite company. But, if you encounter one of *those* wine fans and they back you into a conversational corner, jostling to establish their dominant wine credentials, it's a very nice word to whip out and bang on the table. It'll settle everything down nicely: phenolic. Feel the air in the room contract.

'Phenolics' are a group of compounds found in the grape, most important of which are polyphenols. Polyphenols are powerful antioxidants that exist in grape skins and stems. Some thick-skinned grape varieties are rich in polyphenols, others less so. Anthocyanins are a type of polyphenol. Anthocyanins are the compounds that give grapes (and the resulting wine) their colour. As well as giving bitterness and texture, polyphenol's antioxidant properties help preserve the wine, giving it the ability to age. The more intense the colour in the wine, the more polyphenols, and the more antioxidants! So, red trumps white in this regard.

This antioxidant effect, to a greater or lesser extent, transfers to you when you drink it. This is the major contributor to the 'wine is good for you in small volumes' argument. I don't really want to get into all that; if you're drinking for your health, I think you've probably missed the point. But the fact remains; wine is a fabulous antioxidant.

Back to that great winey word. You might refer to a wine being quite phenolic if it happens to have lots of colour, or other characters you associate with the wine having spent lots of time in contact with the skins. I might use the phrase when talking about a rosé that's a bit richer and darker than the usual.

Tannins

Another polyphenol, and a key contributor to the flavour of wine, specifically the bitterness, is tannin. Tannin exists in the grape skins, seeds and stems predominantly. Tannin is the reason you feel that gripping sensation on your cheeks and gums when drinking big reds. In large quantities it'll have you gurning like your parents in the nineties. In lesser quantities, it adds a sensation of richness and grip; all lovely additional texture, in light reds and some whites, too. Winemakers have a fair amount of sway in how tannic a wine becomes; more on this later.

Tannins develop as the grapes ripen. Cooler climates with less sunshine and lower temperatures at ripening, tend to produce spikier, more raw, grippy tannins; sometimes referred to as 'green' tannins, since they're reminiscent of biting into the grape stems. Warmer climates ripen the tannins more; these ripe tannins feel softer and chewier on the palate, even when the wine has high levels of tannin overall. It's a textural nuance thing. Bite stuff to experience tannins in the wild, deeply coloured raw fruit and veg, for example. Drink reds of different shades from different climates and you'll quite quickly get the lay of the land for yourself.

The Place – Terroir

Terroir (pronounced *tair-wah*) is a big name on campus. It's the central concept in wine, really. Often described gleefully by wine experts to the perceived uninitiated as: 'A very complex thing, made up of myriad slight nuances.' It isn't. It's incredibly easy. Terroir means: 'It tastes like where it comes from. It has a sense of place.'

One of wine's greatest attributes is its ability to hold unique flavours and aromas that have developed over a long season on the vine. The vine itself doesn't move, so year by year, at harvest, its fruit reflects the unique local climate it was exposed to. If it was particularly hot, the fruit will be sweeter; colder, more acidic and less ripe. The resulting wines will follow suit.

The word terroir can be used liberally to describe a particular bottle of wine's sense of place – 'Cor, Jeremy. This is SUCH a terroir wine' – or as a catch-all term for the local environment – 'Let's hop over that vineyard wall and have a butcher's at the terroir, eh?' Terroir could be used to describe a relatively large region – an English county's wines, for example – but not much larger than that. Certainly not a whole country's wines. But it can be used to describe areas as small as single vineyard rows. Burgundy is the spiritual home of terroir and is the poster child for tiny plots of land with demonstrably distinct terroirs. The arbiter of whether a particular plot of land – whatever the size – has a distinct terroir will be whether consistent recurring characteristics are found in the wines, year-in-year-out. It will usually have some defining geological, geographical or cultural characteristics to it that set it apart from its neighbouring plots.

On an individual level, gaining a good perception of the particular terroir of a place – one where you can confidently taste a wine and say, 'This is unusually ripe and rich for a Marsannay' – comes from tasting a wide range of wines from that particular region over a number of years. It also involves remembering roughly what they tasted like. Do this enough and you'll form a perception of 'the norm' and appreciate wines that step outside of it. Each wine you try, bear in mind, will shift the norm or the average a little in your mind; so, the 'typical' terroir of a place is in a constant state of evolution.

A diverse array of factors affects the terroir of a particular place. Some people consider terroir to be solely an environmental thing; the sum of the unique natural environment in which the vine sits. They feel any human intervention, and certainly anything beyond a gentle press of the grapes and a natural fermentation in the winery, is adding character; either masking the terroir in the wine, or adding something harmonious, but ultimately not truly terroir; and so inferior.

I get their point, and I agree environmental factors are the backbone of terroir – in many cases the natural environment is almost the whole picture. But I also feel that the human element, the local tradition and its influence, has a valid contribution to make, too.

Make up your own mind – let your opinion evolve. Whatever you decide 'terroir' is, I think it's helpful to understand, broadly, what each of the various elements brings to the final experience. With this knowledge, you can anticipate the character of a wine from any region before you decide to purchase and crack open the bottle.

Sunshine and Temperature

Put simply, the more sunshine a vine gets, the riper its fruit becomes. This is complicated somewhat by the fact that each grape varietal likes a different amount of sunshine to achieve ripeness. Muscat de Alexandria needs a lot of sun over many months, whereas Pinot Gris can produce quite nicely balanced wines with much less sunshine. So, it's certainly a case of having the right varietal planted in the right place to make sure it gets the right amount of sunshine. But the essential fact remains; the sunnier it is, the riper the fruit.

Riper fruit means juicier, bolder characters in the final wine. Typically, it might mean more opulent aromatics – aromas and flavours heading towards blossom or honeysuckle, ripe melons, that sort of thing. The final sweetness level of a wine is determined largely by how much of the natural sugar the winemaker chooses to leave in the wine after the fermentation. Sunnier wines, whether actually sweeter than others or not, will have a perception of more generous, sweet fruit because of the ripeness. All that extra sugar usually means more alcohol in the final wine. Because of this, they will also have greater body – that rich, full, mouth-filling texture. Riper fruit's acidity will usually be a little lower, so they'll have a softer, rounder, less astringent appeal in the mouth, too.

Conversely, less sun means less of all that stuff above.

Temperature's a funny one. Often assumed to have the same effect as sunshine, in fact, temperature does different things to a wine. It is the warming temperature that largely dictates when the vine leaves winter dormancy and begins to create buds at the start of the year. Higher temperatures develop the anthocyanins in the grape faster, too, so warm areas gain more colour and tannin in the fruit.

Soil

This is the biggest dinner table bore of the lot. Mention 'soil' to a room of casual wine drinkers and hear the palpable sigh of disappointment. Soil. Yawn. But, hear me out. Soil is incredible.

Vines exist in soils of extremes; from pure white chalk and decomposing marine fossils in Chablis and Champagne, to layers of loose rocky slate on slopes so steep you need a harness in the Mosel and vineyards so sandy you need a bucket and spade in Setubal. Vines will grow in almost any soil on the planet. Counter-intuitively, the greatest vineyards often have the poorest nutrient soils. A vine given everything it ever wanted nutrient-wise, without having to work hard for it, swiftly becomes enormous and lazy, spending its days on TikTok and masturbating and strangling things for its own amusement, rather than focussing on ripening its precious fruit to a perfect balance. That's the gist of it anyway.

It is questionable whether chalky soils literally make wines taste chalkier, but many believe it to be true. Many wines grown on mineral-rich soils do indeed taste very 'minerally'. Romantic ideal or yet-to-be-confirmed science, you can jump in at whichever end you fancy. More verifiable is the soil's nutrient density, which will dictate a vine's vigour. Free-draining soils are usually good; less water and fewer nutrients means vines have to grow deeper, with stronger root systems to search for the limited resources. Soils can help to retain heat in warm weather, radiating it back to the vine to aid ripening. And certain vine varieties have a particular affinity for certain soil types.

Soil health is not to be overlooked either. You can tell a generally healthy soil from a sad one with even a layman's look. Look for telltale clues as to the vineyard's commitment to biodiversity and environmental sustainability. Savvy vineyards might plant a mix of biodiverse cover crops between the vines to enrich the soil and bring back lost nutrients; clovers, legumes and wild flowers are common. Organic matter is essential in healthy soils. Look for sheep in the vineyards, trees or other plants growing nearby or within the vineyard, a few weeds here and there isn't a bad thing. Be sceptical of a perfectly manicured, open soil and vine-only vineyard – in most cases, there should be more going on than that.

Altitude and Aspect

The higher up you go, the cooler it gets. That's the general rule. For every hundred metres higher you go, the temperature drops by about 1°C. So, if you're looking to make wine in a cooler climate, it helps to plant higher; this is a hugely important consideration today with global warming. Vineyards in the warmest wine regions in the world are migrating up nearby hills to reduce the impact of rising temperatures.

High altitude is a major contributor to why countries usually considered 'hot', like Argentina, Chile and Australia, are able to make lighter, fresher styles of wines than you might expect. So, as well as questioning how warm the country is, it helps to ask, 'Is it grown up a hill?', too.

The term 'aspect' refers to the angle of the slope on which a vineyard is planted. There are vineyards planted on very flat plains, but most have some degree of slope. Currently, and for many centuries, the steepest vineyards in the world are in the Bremmer Calmont area of Germany's Mosel Valley, with vines planted on sixty-five-degree slopes overlooking the Mosel River.

Aspect is important for many reasons. In the northern hemisphere, a southerly exposure with a steep aspect will achieve maximum sunlight, which can be very helpful in ripening fruit in cool wine regions. Equally, north-facing slopes will reduce sun exposure in hot winemaking regions, which may be just as useful. In the Northern hemisphere, the opposite applies: Northern exposure gets more sun, southerly more shade.

Aspect helps with water run-off in wet seasons and is an enormously important protection against severe frosts in cool climates. Frost can cling to the ground, and cold air slides downhill while warm air rises, so planting on slopes helps to move frosts to the bottom of the hill as warm air currents come up the other way.

Lastly, more extreme aspects make using machinery very hard. So, vineyards on a proper tilt require hand labour vine-by-vine. This is undoubtably a 'better' way to do it, in terms of quality and romanticism, but it is much more expensive and time-consuming. So, steep vineyards are labours of passion and ambition, rather than commercial cash cows.

Local Ecosystem

Just as soils impart a unique character to the vine's fruit, local biodiversity and specific qualities of the ecosystem in and around the vineyard often appear to have a profound impact on the final wine.

An example is the 'garrigue' tasting note, usually associated with France's southern Rhône, Provence or Languedoc wines. It's used to describe herbaceous, lightly spicy, earthy characters that are found in the wine. These are reminiscent of the scrub and famous herbs that grow wild in the hot, dry, Mediterranean region, known as garrigue.

This element of terroir fascinates me, as it's often unclear whether this is pure placebo, based on seeing or reading about the local environment and putting two and two together. It may simply be wine trade legend, passed down from one generation of wine professional to another, so it becomes 'the correct thing to say' when tasting a particular wine. However, it might also be true that the local herbs do pass on character in a way we do not yet appreciate. It could also be only partly true; perhaps the local herbs themselves don't pass their flavour directly to the grapes, but there are chemical compounds in the wines that do, indeed, combine to give a similar character . . .

Saline breezes blowing across vineyards in coastal areas routinely appear to transfer a salty tang to the wines made nearby. Again, this isn't as scientific as you might hope – there is a debate about whether it is indeed the proximity to the sea that brings salt to the wine (sea spray landing on skins close to harvest for example) or whether the sensation of saltiness is actually derived from more saline minerals in the soil, which are drawn into the vine through its uptake of water. While I do find some minerally whites grown inland to have a salty line, in my experience, the majority do have coastal locations. Try the white wines of Spain's Rías Baixas or Greece's Santorini as good examples. Let the ideas percolate with you and you can draw your own position.

Local Tradition and Human Culture

This is the bit of the terroir chat that carries some strong, polarised opinion and fosters great debate. Depending on your particular vibe, humans might not contribute to terroir but, if you're like me, they might well do.

The natural environment comes together to create wines of unique character. Worms wiggle and perform their duties. Rabbits and deer and badgers and owls strut about shouting and biting each other, rubbing up against things and nibbling whatever they fancy. As a wild boar scratches an itch on a row of Garnacha vines, far up a mountain in Spain, just as its parents and grandparents did before it, it is, I imagine, largely uninterested in its profound impact on the terroir of the resulting wines. But, as its wiry exterior rubs young spring buds from the vine, it dramatically reduces the potential yields of the vineyard and, therefore, the resulting wine's character. Humans do this, too, except we have eloquence and lipstick and cash to persuade others to rub the buds for us.

The human hand is especially important to a wine's terroir in regions where techniques have formed part of the local tradition. How vines are trained – whether on a pergola overhead, low to the ground in little basket shapes, or in neat rows – makes a big difference to the wine. Hand harvesting or using machinery has an impact on fruit quality and quantity. Green harvesting, removing some bunches before ripening to make the remaining fruit more concentrated and ripe, and irrigating or dry farming vines without watering – these are just a few examples of the human decisions that can be every bit as impactful on the local wines as the natural elements.

Overly tweaked wines, which have been made to fit a commercial style, arguably lose their terroir. When work in the winery is gentle and considerate of the natural character of the fruit, then I think it's the opposite; winery techniques can *add* to a wine's terroir. Allowing indigenous yeasts in the natural environment to perform the fermentation arguably preserves and adds unique terroir nuances to the wine, compared to using commercially cultured yeasts. The use, or not, of local or traditionally sourced oak, where this has been historically important, has an impact.

Since Roman times, vines have criss-crossed Europe and, latterly, they've travelled the world, finding exciting, new homes and becoming part of the local flavour. Each new home offers a blank canvas on which to paint the local terroir. Terroir can be at its most exciting with vines indigenous to their area, being grown as closely to nature as possible, and made in a traditional style – a terroir expression going back centuries. Equally, terroir can be a snapshot of the current moment. New varieties and techniques creating non-traditional wines that give just as much raw experience to the drinker. The terroir of today; a region on the move. I love both expressions.

The key thing is that each wine has its own unique terroir. It's trying to show you something. Trying to get its point across. Take a moment to listen to what it has to say. Not literally, you'll get strange looks and be refused a second glass. I mean, try to empty your mind before you swirl and sniff a wine for the first time. Before you inevitably engage brain and start to use this marvellous wine knowledge you hold to make sense of it, allow your first sensations of the wine to be pure. You'll be surprised at how emotive, how memory-inducing, how much of a sensation of unique personality you'll find if you do. This is my favourite, always brief, moment of trying a wine. The analytical bit anyone can do with a bit of practice.

2.

How Wine Is Made

The actual act of winemaking has made an appearance in previous chapters but only as a bit-part protagonist compared with nature's unimpeachable processes. In my eagerness to share the pure majesty of wine's 'natural' concepts, like fermentation and terroir, I've skirted close to undermining the skill (nay art!) of winemaking. I've climbed proverbial stacks of fine oak barrels in muddy outdoor boots, only to loud hailer the virtues of letting the vineyard do the talking. *Christ, he's hamming it up now*. I've given well-meaning winemakers a disapproving stare, helicoptering wine-filled hoses above my head, while wearing a single vine leaf –*that's quite enough, Tom!* – just to make my point that nature is important.

Now let's get some balance back. Great wines can be all about the vineyard, sure. But great wines can also be about the winery. And the best wines are where both reach total harmony. It can be easy to fall into the modern wine trap of being dogmatic about the virtues of minimalism and 'low intervention' winemaking. This current trend is itself a push back against the previous fashion, a decade or more ago, for very poked and prodded, bold wines. It will swing round again, no doubt. Environmental and social responsibility considered, I heartily recommend you drink as widely in style, price point, scale of producer and production method as you can. You may well love lower-alcohol, minimal-intervention wines, but how will you know unless you've had a decent crack at some gigantic, bull-in-a-china-shop powerhouses, too?

Big flavour and bold character can be too much, while elegant and finely structured wines can be extraordinarily boring without enough nuance and interest tied into them. Winemaking is about trying to find a perfect balance; the greatest possible expression of the fruit. Every press, every fermentation is an opportunity to coax gently, or not so gently, the juice into achieving its full potential.

In its simplest form, winemaking is a very pure, straight-line process from grape to bottle. The general idea is that the grapes are picked at optimum ripeness, as delicately as possible, brought into a winery and pressed relatively gently to extract juice. The grape juice's natural sugars are fermented by yeasts to create alcohol. And there you have wine. But there's a bit more to it than that, and many options are available to the winemaker to change the course of the journey, so let's follow the process from start to finish, taking the scenic route.

The Roots

Most wine drinkers would assume that *vitis vinifera* vines are simply planted in the soil. Traditionally, this would have been the case. Some still are, but it's rare. Unfortunately, a pest called phylloxera has made it nearly impossible. Vines now require a work-around. Let's explain . . .

Phylloxera is an aphid native to America. As an adult it has wings and can fly, making it hugely mobile and able to travel long distances quickly. As larvae, it enjoys nibbling *vitis vinifera* roots. It is so good at this, it kills the vine from the roots up very swiftly. Phylloxera first arrived in Europe in the 1800s, via plants being imported from America. By the early 1900s, it had wiped out the vast majority of Europe's grape vines. The wine world was on its knees.

The interesting thing is, having grown up with phylloxera present, American *vitis* species (*vitis labrusca*, *vitis riparia*, etc.) are immune to its evil ways. A plan was hatched to save Europe's vines by 'grafting' European *vitis vinifera* varieties on to American vine roots. Grafting is a skilful technique of attaching one plant to another, so they grow to become one plant. One end of the plant is *vitis vinifera* and the other is *vitis* 'whatever you choose'.

The American vine roots planted in European vineyards provide full protection from phylloxera and are known as 'root stocks'. The European vines grafted to them just above the soil line grow perfectly well and retain their distinct varietal character. Nowadays, winemakers even select specific types of root stock to best match the soil.

This clever technique allowed Europe's vineyards, and latterly, the world's, since phylloxera travelled everywhere over the following century, to be replanted and it saved the wine industry. Today, it is standard practice. There are some vines that are still un-grafted, in areas where phylloxera is uncommon or has never been observed, but they are fascinating anomalies rather than the norm.

FUN FACT: a sudden lack of brandy in England, due to French vineyards dying, caused social elites to seek an alternative tipple. Roll up, Scotch whisky. Without phylloxera, Scotch and other whiskies may not have had the cherished place in our hearts that they do today.

The Vineyard Cycle

Vines follow an annual cycle, the end result of which, if all goes to plan, is a single crop of nice ripe grapes.

Winter

Vines have a winter dormancy period. The leaves drop off. The vine builds its carbohydrate reserves and stores up its energy for the coming year in the trunk; the largest part of the vine's body rising out of the ground. During this time, the shoots and canes coming off the trunk, from last year's growth, become darker wood and harden. These leafless, skeletal vineyards have a special feel and are very different to the lush flora of the main season. They are quieter, ethereal spots. Magical places. The vineyard team will prune these one-year-old shoots back during the winter period, neatening up the vine and preparing it for the coming year's growing season.

There are many different ways to train a vine in a vineyard, each suited to different environmental and geological scenarios. Some vines are left relatively wild but, even these usually get a little nudge in the right direction with some secateurs. This winter pruning is enormously important. It is the winemaker's opportunity to shape the vine and keep it happy and well-balanced; the perfect size and shape for its specific environment. It's not just about the vine's health and happiness, though. Considered pruning can help establish the height of the 'fruiting zone' (where the grape bunches grow), often allowing vines to be picked more easily by hand. It's helpful if getting at the grapes doesn't require huge amounts of bending down or reaching high overhead! Well-planned pruning also helps moderate the risk of vine diseases. It can even keep the coming year's buds away from the worst of the nasty spring frosts.

The general idea, whatever the pruning style adopted by the winemaker, is to create the healthiest platform from which the new season's shoots can grow and to remove any undesired wood that would only serve to cause the vine nutrient stress and get in the way. Winemakers will often keep a small number (one or two, typically) of the shoots from last year's growth and remove the rest. These retained one-year-old shoots will have a number of 'nodes', small lumps from where buds will spring. The shoots are typically trained using trellising wires to grow horizontally out from the vine like an outstretched arm. When spring comes and buds start opening and new shoots start growing, they are then able to grow vertically, straight up, in nice, neat rows. But there are many ways to prune and train, as I say – each vineyard is unique.

As the weather warms up and spring comes along, the nodes burst into life with small buds becoming quick-growing green shoots. They rise up vertically, if trained to do so, or sprawl out in all directions, if left 'wild'. Leaves and inflorescences (groups of flowers that will become grapes in due course) develop swiftly and within a few weeks of 'budburst' (the moment buds start to open up), the vineyard is once again filled with verdant life. The flowers are pollinated (with almost all winemaking vines being hermaphroditic) and by early summer the vines have sparse, bright green, little bunches of grapes forming. Tiny, rock-hard, caper-sized grapes gently swell and, as they do, they grow closer together forming bunches. They are building sugars and their natural acidities are softening as they ripen and moving closer with every moment in the sunshine to perfect ripeness.

By mid-summer, almost all grape varieties will have begun to take on colour. Where all grapes start as small, green, little things, white-skinned grapes become more translucent as they ripen, while black-skinned grapes get more deeply coloured as they grow. There is a wider spectrum of grape colour than the two poles of white and black, however, and *gris*, for example, refers to the grey, light pink hues often found on grapes of these varieties.

Grapes reach full ripeness at different times. Varieties can have a shorter, or longer, ripening cycle. In general, harvests start in late August in the northern hemisphere and run through to around October. In the southern hemisphere, harvest runs from late January to April. In both hemispheres, some rare, late-harvest wine styles mean harvest can stretch for a month or more beyond these times. Equally, with global warming, some varietals are being picked earlier.

Late Summer into Autumn

Winemakers are paying close attention to their vines through-out the year, but especially close attention begins in the month or so running up to harvest. In the weeks before, regular samples are taken from across the vineyard to help establish sugar and acidity levels in the grapes. These are the key indicators of when a vine is ready to pick. Winemakers are looking for enough sugar to produce the desired level of alcohol, but are equally desperate to retain enough natural acidity to ensure the wines are limber and well-balanced. Regular checks allow a winemaker to assess how swiftly the ripening is happening and to book in a team to pick the fruit on just the right day.

That's the dream, anyway. In reality, of course, the freelance or agency pickers might be on another job, or it might be their day off, so winemakers book them pre-emptively months in advance for a date they feel might be right, then at the last minute a dance occurs with winemakers across the region calling the picking teams to try to renegotiate. 'Yes, I know I expected to need you Friday next week, but Monday was super-sunny!' 'Oh, Sergio has you booked in, eh? His vineyard's cooler than mine, I'll call him and try to swap.'

Picking by hand is great – it's what we all expect. Teams of pickers moving down rows of vines, shears in hand, jauntily filling baskets with ripe fruit. That is genuinely the vibe for a lot of wine. It's nice work for a bit. Then it gets bloody samey, to be honest. If you try it, I'd pick a cool climate to avoid the snakes and spiders you find elsewhere! The benefit of 'hand harvesting' is that it allows for individual inspection of bunches as you pick. Any rot or other negative stuff occurring can be avoided and only pristine grapes go in the basket. The down-side is it's expensive, hugely labour intensive and, as mentioned before, you have to align your pickers' diaries with your vineyards, which is easier said than done. So, many wines are picked using machinery instead. It's quicker and the machines are always available the moment you need them. It's cheaper (once you've paid off your harvester) and, increasingly, the machines are more and more gentle, so there's not a dramatic decline in quality of picked fruit. The snag with machinery is that it's naff all use on steep slopes. So, if your vineyard stands proudly on the banks of a beautiful river, like the Mosel, then your only option is to go and do the work by hand.

Horses for courses – don't assume a wine is crap if it's machine harvested and vice versa. What is a good sign, though, if you're visiting a vineyard near harvest, is if the winemaker really 'knows' their fruit. Let yourself be confident if they're tasting grapes as they wander the vineyards. Ideally, they're spitting chewed grapes into their hand and looking at the colour of the pips intently, chewing the skins a bit and making a slight squinty face and staring off into the middle distance. That sort of thing. Buy that wine.

A very loose visualisation of vineyard cycles in Northern and Southern hemispheres

NORTHERN HEMISPHERE

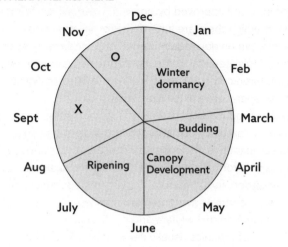

SOUTHERN HEMISPHERE

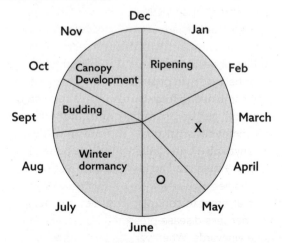

X = Typical harvest dates   O = Late harvest styles

Organic Wine

Like other organic products, organic wine is grown within the defined standards of law (the EU has defined organic standards, for example) and approved by one of the organic certification bodies, of which there are a number. Certification bodies may have their own unique requirements for a producer above the minimum legislated standards, but fundamentally each has the same basic criteria. A good example is The Soil Association, which has been active since the 1960s.

Organic production bans man-made chemicals, allowing only specific, naturally occurring compounds to be used in controlled quantities. Proponents of organics promote it as being the only formally legislatively controlled sustainable farming method and, therefore, transparent and measurable. At its best, it certainly promotes environmentally positive farming, higher animal welfare and biodiversity.

Criticism of organics usually centres around it being considered challenging to do for many commercial businesses in colder, wetter, more fungal-disease-prone places, like the UK. Organics comes at an increased cost, not least paying for certification, so products are sold to consumers at a premium price. There is also some argument that the unnaturally high concentrations of naturally occurring compounds used as fungicides or herbicides in organics, such as copper or sulphur (sometimes combined to form inorganic and hotly debated copper-sulphate), can be just as toxic and potentially damaging to the environment as small quantities of man-made chemicals.

As with anything, I think there's nuance in there. Spraying shedloads of anything is a bad idea and I'd like to think certification bodies regularly review their standards and legislation to attempt to control it. Organics is certainly 'easier' in drier, warmer, less-disease-pressured places, like Argentina's high-altitude vineyards. Wherever grapes are grown, I'm pro fewer chemicals of any kind and I do like to champion those winemakers trying their best by the environment, their team and their customer.

Can you taste the 'organic' in wine? No. You're not paying a premium for that. Some organic wines are fantastic, others are not. You're paying a premium to support the organic movement on environmental grounds. Examples of organic producers to check out are: Emiliana in Chile; Torres in Spain and Chile; Oxney in England; and Domaine Gayda in France. There are loads.

Biodynamic Wine

Biodynamics seeks to connect the scientific understanding of the natural world with the spiritual. Like organics, it eschews man-made chemicals entirely, but goes further; limiting the farmer to nine highly specific natural preparations used at different times within the agricultural cycle. Preparations tend to be plant-based (chamomile, yarrow, dandelion, nettle, etc.), finely ground quartz silica, or the fan-favourite – manure aged underground in hollow cow horns. Each is used in homoeopathically small doses that are aimed at supporting the natural defences and rhythms of the ecosystem. Often, these preparations are applied according to the lunar calendar, with certain days being defined as root, leaf, flower or fruit days, and specific activity being carried out on the relevant day.

Biodynamics promotes a biodiverse, closed-loop system of farming, where animals are kept to provide manure and the farmer never takes more from the land than they put back in. In this way, it is a more holistic system than organics. It does have certification bodies, for example, Demeter, but they are not defined in law in the same way. Some producers follow the full doctrine to the letter, others pick and choose certain elements that they feel are beneficial. Biodynamics is used by many very well-known wine producers. Many of the most expensive and iconic names in wine are biodynamic, for example, Alsace's Zind-Humbrecht, Domaine Michel Lafarge and Domaine de la Romanée-Conti in Burgundy, Italy's Querciabella, and Seña in Chile.

Critics point to the absence of scientific justification for the methods and philosophy. Much like organics, it is also commercially challenging if the wines are not at a premium price point. Some advocates ignore the more spiritual elements but suggest that being actively present in your vineyards more often, which is what comes with non-chemical farming like this, creates better wine in and of itself.

Personally, I find biodynamics fascinating. I think I can go without the dogma and pseudoscientific origins and still be amazed at the quality of wines that are sometimes made in this way. I am in awe of the bravery and determination of producers who use biodynamics to be better connected with their land, support biodiversity and promote regeneration of the ecosystem, rather than chasing ever-more commercial growth and higher yields.

Regenerative Viticulture

Increasingly given the spotlight, regenerative viticulture is a modern farming system. It seeks to be a toolbox for producers who want to work more holistically with nature. It often incorporates many of the same practices and principles as organics and biodynamics but without the dogma and strict rules.

Farming regeneratively means to leave the vineyard in a better condition than when you began. Practices focus on boosting soil's organic matter, fertility and increasing the levels of microbial life beneath the ground. Typically, producers will not till their soil, instead leaving the ground unbroken to preserve crucial fungal networks that allow plants and other fauna to communicate and share nutrient resources. Purveyors reduce or totally eschew chemical use, although it is not 'banned' as in other doctrines. There is minimal use of heavy machinery, so as not to compact the soil. Biodiverse crops are planted throughout the vineyards, agroforestry is promoted, so it isn't just vine after vine for miles around. This helps with water retention and promotes wildlife, attracting beneficial insects and creating natural ecosystems. It recommends that animals graze the land – cover crops provide food for the animals and they, in turn, provide manure. Minimal wastage and use of composts is common, too.

While it is relatively new, it feels to me that regenerative agriculture, including viticulture, has a lot of potential. I'm excited at the prospect of its proliferation and seeing if it can truly help us reduce reliance on chemicals and improve our impact on nature. Examples of producers championing regenerative viticulture are Everflyht in England, Maison Mirabeau in Provence and Hope Well Wine in Oregon.

In the Winery

Picked grapes tend to be packed into shallow crates. Everything is organised to avoid the grapes getting squashed, as the moment you break the skin, oxygen begins to degrade the fruit and rot sets in quickly. Powdered sulphur, working as an antioxidant, is often sprinkled over the grapes to protect them on their (hopefully) short journey to the winery. The shorter the time between picking and pressing, the better, and the less need for sulphur.

The winery receives pallets stacked high with these small crates. They're the perfect size and shape to be picked up by a winemaker and tossed into a press, crusher, de-stemmer or sorting table, depending on the winery's process. It's manual work a lot of the time. In big, commercial operations, it's more automated.

On the fresh grapes' arrival to the winery, the winemaking process can go in multiple directions, depending on the style of wine being produced.

Specific wine regions (Burgundy, Bordeaux, Tuscany, you name it) have certification bodies that oversee all wines made in their region. They come armed with a set of winemaking rules laid down in law, which stipulate the parameters that the winemaker needs to play within to use the official regional name on the label. Typically, the rules will stipulate the limited geographical area of growing and production, the allowable winery processes and the specific grape varietals that it is possible to use. They may have other requirements, like how long a wine must be aged before it can be sold for example. Each region has its own set of rules, developed around its unique climate and regional culture over time. This means there is a strong degree of conformity within established wine regions the world over.

There are, of course, winemakers who do not conform in these regions – and, by and large, a winemaker can do whatever they like in pursuit of the best vinous expression of their land, whether the regional certification rules allow it or not. It just means they won't be able to put the protected regional name like 'Chablis' or 'Chianti' on the label . . . which is a bit of a pain when it comes to marketing and selling the wine, to say the least.

If it sounds like I'm slightly pushing against the regulations at all, I'm not. For the most part, they exist to ensure quality, protect regional identity and the winemaking tradition. They also help consumers have a pretty good idea of what they're getting when they buy a wine. Which is no bad thing. Up to a point.

Making White, Rosé and Red Wine

At its most simple, there are three key colours of wine, right? That's a nice way to sort them. White, rosé, red. Banked.

Within each of these three 'colours' there is a spectrum from lighter to darker examples, which often correlate to the fresher wines and the heavier, richer wines out there. Most wines we meet day-to-day sit quite happily in this merry trio. Wine being wine, though, there are an extraordinary number of potential variations and styles of wine across the world that challenge the perceived boundaries of these three colour categories. This is ultimately what makes wine so exploratory and joyful. Where does dark rosé end and light red begin, for example? Does it matter?

Occasionally, one of these outliers breaks into the mainstream consciousness for a bit. Orange wine is the latest example. If I didn't mention it, half the sommeliers in East London would be stamping their latest-season Crocs and yelling, 'Hey, there're four key colours of wine, mate! Don't dismiss orange! Oraange!' Well, they can cease ruffling their French-blue overshirts and rippling those perfectly waxed moustaches and relax. We'll cover the auburn trustafarian and all those like it here, too. We're going to look at how to make fortified wine and, of course, sparkling wine, as well.

But, before we kick the winery door off its hinges and conga around the weird, wonderful and more unconventional elements of the winemaking world, let's set the scene by looking at how our key three colours are made, as a basic standard . . .

White

White wines can start life as white or black grapes. For the vast majority, it's white grapes.

The grapes are pressed gently, with juice having little or no contact with the grape skins as it runs off the press, so the juice remains clear. This clear juice is then fermented without the skins, meaning it retains the fresh, 'clean' grape-juice characteristics, rather than picking up the more complex, bitter qualities that the skins add.

Rosé

Rosé is made from black grapes but sometimes has white grapes in the mix, too.

The grapes are pressed gently, with minimal contact between the skins and the pressed juice. The colour in rosé and red wines comes from the amount of time the clear juice has in contact with the skins. Rosé simply has less time than red wines, so extracting less colour and less bitter characters. Lighter rosés usually have less skin contact time; darker rosés more skin contact time. Thicker-skinned, darker grapes give more colour and require less contact time than thinner-skinned varieties.

Rosés tend to be fermented without skins present. So, typically, the skins are removed from the juice before fermentation begins.

Red

Red wines must be made from black grapes. They are almost always made entirely from black grapes. However, a small quantity of white grapes can sometimes be added to the blend in relatively rare examples.

The grapes tend to be crushed down with the skins left fully in contact with the resulting juice. The juice and skins receive extended periods of contact time. This draws out colour, bitter tannins and additional flavour.

Fermentation takes place with the skins still in contact with the juice. The longer the skins remain in contact, the richer and darker the wine becomes. Fermentation naturally warms the wine; this heat draws more colour and tannin out of the skins.

After fermentation, the skins are filtered out of the now-red wine.

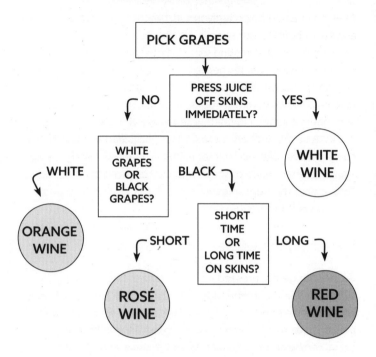

The Nuances of Winemaking

Now, that's the basics but, as mentioned before, wine is a vast, swirling, creative process. Every winery uses subtly differing techniques; there is a diverse range of tweaks and pathways available for a winemaker to subtly (or not so subtly) coax the wine in the direction they're aiming. There are decisions to be made at every stage of the process that will have a profound impact on the final wine.

For the drinker, knowing a little more about these winemaking techniques and the decisions made in the winery, helps us assess whether the bottle in our hands is likely to be the right one to buy. On tasting a wine, knowing a few of the nuances of its production helps us work out where the range of aromas and flavours filling our senses may be derived.

Getting good at tasting wine is largely a memory game. Knowing a wine was fermented in French oak, and remembering the sensation this gave on the nose and palate when you tasted it, allows you to recognise that sensation when you encounter it again. Do it a few times and it'll stick.

So, let's follow the winemaking process and explore the common avenues available at each key stage. As we go, you'll learn the effect each of these processes has on the final wine and acquire the right questions to ask to gain the understanding you want before you buy!

Squashing the Grapes

Grapes are gently pressed or crushed to extract the juice. Whatever the technique, the general idea is to extract the best juice possible and to avoid breaking the little pips. Within the pips and stems of a grape bunch, there are enormously bitter characters waiting to leap out into the wine – we don't want 'em in it. Before fermentation, this pressed grape juice is known as 'must'.

The most common approach for whites, rosés and some reds is to de-stem the bunches before they go in the press, so you are just pressing the grapes themselves. The grapes are popped into a press and pressure is applied to extract the juice gently, which then drains into a vat waiting below. This process allows the juice a little time in contact with the skins before they are removed, if desired, and de-stemming also allows for the maximum possible pressure to be applied – to extract a little more juice – without getting too many bitter notes.

Almost all grapes have clear juice – you can see this when you bite into one and its flesh inside is clear. A very, very small number of black grapes do have coloured juice, actually . . . but they are rare. Known as Teinturier, the French term for the person who dyes clothing, these grapes are the exception to the rule that the colour for rosé and red wines comes only from the skins. Check out Alicante Bouschet as an example of this.

Typically, the standard process for red wines is to de-stem the grapes, as with whites and rosés, then crush them. In 'crushing', the grapes are blitzed to create a rugged soup of black grape skin fragments and juice. These are fermented together to give maximum opportunity for the colours and flavours and bitter notes to be extracted from the skins into the juice.

You don't have to de-stem, though; many white wines, rosés and some reds are pressed as whole bunches of grapes, stems and all. The stems can help extract the juice more quickly and cleanly than if they were not present, as they create little channels within the 'marc' (the pressed grapes) for the juice to run off. As the pressing is gentle and the time that the juice is in contact with the stems is very brief, little colour or bitterness is transferred. Whole-bunch pressing is in many ways the 'original' method – before de-stemming machines, everyone did it – and it tends to lead to more elegant, finer-structured wines as a large generalisation. Also, the pressing pressures are lower for whole bunches, to avoid extracting bitter notes from breaking down the stems.

'Whole bunch' reds are quite trendy at the moment – often exalted for their clarity and purity of fruit flavour. The pressed whole bunches – skins, stems and all – are added to the fermentation vessel to ferment as red wine classically would. The stems do add a subtle stalky, green quality, sometimes a little spice note and often an extra bitter character. This can be beneficial in thinner-skinned, lighter-bodied black grapes, like Pinot Noir, to add a bit of texture. Conversely, some winemakers use this gentler, whole-bunch-pressing technique in order to extract less richness and weight from their thick-skinned, bold-flavoured black grape varieties.

A quick segue on carbonic maceration . . . You may well encounter wines made using a process called carbonic maceration. Beaujolais is the heartland of this style but it's used to great effect all over the world. It is a process where whole bunches of grapes are placed into a tank without pressing. The tank is closed, made airtight and flushed with carbon dioxide. In this oxygen-free environment, fermentation begins within each individual grape. After a period of time, the winemaker presses these grapes to extract the semi-fermented juice, then completes fermentation in the standard way. This process leads to extra-juicy, bright-fruited, sometimes floral and aromatic characters in the resulting wine, with lower bitterness and tannin.

Skin Contact

Once the juice has been extracted, the winemaker can choose whether to give the skins and juice time in touch with each other before fermentation begins.

Many white wines have little or no skin contact at this point. However, the winemaker may let the juice and skins mingle about at a cool temperature for a few hours or even more for some aromatic varieties, or in cases where they want to emphasise the grape's natural fruity aroma and flavour (bold, fragrant Sauvignon Blancs are popularly made like this). This process can add a little density and richness on the palate, too, as it causes more of those polyphenols (mentioned in Chapter 1) to be extracted. This process is sometimes used to prepare wines built to age in a cellar for a long time. Little in the way of colour is extracted from the white grape skins during this time, though, since it is being done at a cool temperature.

This 'pre-soak' at cool temperatures is used in rosé and red wine production very commonly for the same reasons. The length of time can vary dramatically from a few hours to a few days, and even a week or more in some cases. Some colour will be gently extracted from black grapes. In many rosés, this will be the only skin contact they receive to give them their pink hue.

Fermentation

After the desired period of 'pre-soaking' (or not, as the case may be), the pressed juice is ready for fermentation. If it's a white wine, the skins will be removed before fermentation begins, and the same goes for most rosés. However, the skins remain in the juice during fermentation with red wines, or for part of the duration for some rosés.

Then there's the orange wine business . . . These occur when white wines are given extended skin contact during the fermentation process and beyond, like a red wine, but using white grapes only. Keeping the skins in the juice while it ferments gives them a more tannic (grippy) structure and denser flavours. They can be fantastic and represent an interesting category that's well worth exploring. As ever, there's a wide variety of styles out there, ranging from very light with just a bit of extra texture and richness (little skin contact), all the way through to super-tannic, dark amber wines that require chewing through. All of them can be great and there's a time and a place for each one.

Skins or no skins, the juice requires some yeast to kick off fermentation. This can be introduced by inoculating the juice with a commercial strain (controlled, sensible) or letting the wild yeasts in the environment do the job (less controlled, potentially more fun!). Fermentation can take anywhere from a few days to a few weeks, depending on the temperature of the must, the yeast strains used and the amount of sugar being converted. There are some rare examples, usually super-sweet wines like Tokaji Essencia, where fermentation can take years!

The cooler the temperature, the longer fermentation takes and, usually, the more fruity, crisp, clean characters are retained in the final wine. Warmer fermentations are faster and usually create richer, fuller styles of wine. Too cool and fermentation won't start as the yeasts will be inactive; too warm and the wine will have 'cooked' aromas and be quite neutral and boring. A cool fermentation would be between 7°C and 16°C (the typical range for whites); a warm fermentation would be between 20°C and 30°C (the typical range for reds). Most modern wineries have very good temperature control for their winemaking, in order to keep their fermenting wines within the prime range, and this is much easier to achieve in stainless steel tanks, as opposed to other formats, such as wooden barrels.

The Winemaking Vessel

All this is taking place in a water-tight vessel of some sort, of course. From the moment the grapes have been pressed and the juice extracted, the wine has been contained in something. What this vessel is made from, though, could be any number of different things. From clay amphorae to the finest French oak barrels, from stainless steel and rectangular granite tanks to concrete eggs. Many wines start their journey in one type of vessel, only to be moved to another in order to mature.

One thing that every vessel will have in common (in good wine), is that it will be clean. Wineries are exceptionally clean places. It's important, as dirty wineries mean less precise and pristine wines. Small inconsistencies in cleanliness can lead to enormous faults and off-characters in the wines as they move through the winemaking process. I have heard numerous winemakers, all over world, make a quip along the lines of, 'The job is twenty per cent winemaking, eighty per cent cleaning . . .' It's true.

There are two key things at play when it comes to vessels. Firstly, whether the material imparts any additional flavours to the wine. Secondly, whether it is porous and allows a proportion of oxygen ingress, or if it's completely sealed.

Oxygen degrades the wine, so it's important it's kept in check. However, all wines get a little oxygen in them occasionally, otherwise they can become reductive – where they develop a nasty, eggy, sulphury smell and the fruit characters reduce dramatically. Most wines, though, are made with minimal oxygen contact, as this preserves the clean, bright fruit and aromatic notes. Too much oxygen and the wines darken in colour, losing their fresh, fruity character and develop nutty, dried-leaf aromas. Not ideal.

Commonly used winemaking vessels and their key attributes:

Stainless-steel Tanks
These come in every shape and size. They can be bespoke and made to fit the available space in a winery, and are hugely space efficient if you have high ceilings, as they can be incredibly tall and stacked on top of each other with relative ease. They're also very useful things for winemakers who want to make precise, technically correct wines, as they are totally inert (the stainless steel provides no additional flavour to the wine), and are easy to keep flushed with carbon dioxide, argon or another gas to protect the wine from oxygen. Many stainless-steel tanks also have highly efficient temperature controls, allowing winemakers to keep fermentations and finished wines stored for long periods at the ideal temperature. Visit a huge winery and you'll be shocked at how a vast expanse of stainless-steel tanks, as far as the eye can see, can be controlled by a single iPad or tablet. The potential efficiencies and level of control that stainless steel brings to modern wineries is awesome.

Wooden Barrels
These are the romantically charged, beautiful icons of the winery. Evocative and inspiring. Crafted by the hands of a cooper, a barrel is made from long wooden staves (the body), two heads (the circular pieces at each end), and held together

with metal hoops. A bunghole in the middle gives access to the wine inside, with a wooden or silicone bung to stopper it when required. They come in a wide range of sizes, from the classic barrique (traditionally 225 litres in Bordeaux and 228 litres in Burgundy, confusingly), to the enormous foudre made in sizes of up to about 30,000 litres!

Barrels impart distinctive flavour and texture to the wines inside; the porous wood allows the wine to soak into it and draw out its natural woody aromatics and some woody tannins, too. Barrels are 'toasted' with fire when they are first built, and winemakers can choose to have heavier or lighter toasting. The heavier the toasting, the more 'oaky' flavour and aroma the barrel imparts. Barrels can be reused many, many times and last for years (decades!) with good care. As a barrel is used year after year, it gradually reduces the amount of 'oaky' character it imparts, so once it's been filled and used two or three times, the effect becomes more subtle. The porous nature of the barrel also allows a little oxygen to interact with the wine inside. The oxygen gently buffs the tense edges of the young wine, making it feel silkier and smoother in texture when drunk, and slowly maturing the vibrant fruit flavours.

Oak is the most commonly used wood to make wine barrels. Most barrels come from France or the USA. French oak tends to have lower levels of lactones (a key contributor to the oaky flavour) and impart more gentle influence on the wine inside. Typically, French oak barrels give wines subtly spicy characters and a silky, fine texture. American oak imparts more lactones and allows slightly more oxygen interaction, the result is a more obvious 'oaky' character, with elements of butterscotch, popcorn and vanilla, and a creamy texture. Oak barrels from Hungary, Slovenia and other countries are widely used, too. It is relatively rare nowadays to find barrels made from any wood other than oak, but they do occasionally crop up, for example chestnut.

Whatever the wood used, each time a barrel is refilled with new wine, the wood's aromatic potency is diluted. An older, much-used barrel is a very special thing, imparting very subtle nuances, largely adding texture and weight rather than flavour.

A big definer of the way oak presents itself in a finished wine is the size of the barrel being used; smaller barrels hold a greater proportion of the wine in direct contact with the wood, so the oak imparts more character more quickly to the wine. The larger the barrel, the greater the volume of wine inside that is not in direct contact with the wood, so the 'oaky' development is slower and some say, more balanced. The type of oak used and the level of toasting all play their part, too.

Each grape variety interacts with oak differently, some more pleasingly than others. Highly aromatic varieties with big personality (like Sauvignon Blanc and Riesling) tend to get along less well with oak compared to more muted varieties (like Chardonnay). Although there are always notable exceptions. The level of ripeness of the grape variety also has a distinct effect on the oak's integration. Riper, more sweet fruit with lower acidity tends to show oak more visibly and vivaciously in the final wine than a lean, fresh base.

Local Stone

This is a traditional material for winemaking vessels. The type of local stone used changes around the world, of course. I first saw this in Rías Baixas in Galicia, northwest Spain, where the natural, large chunks of granite in the soils are used to form beautiful granite tanks. They also build the end-posts of the vineyard rows out of granite. How the stone affects the wine differs depending on the stone but, taking the granite example, they talk about its wood-like porousness, which allows the wine to breathe a little and evaporate very slowly to gain concentration, richness and weight as it develops. The stone does not itself impart any flavour.

Concrete

A surprisingly good material for making wine vessels. There is
a long history of using concrete in places like the Douro Valley
in Portugal, where they press the grapes and often start the
initial fermentations in large concrete swimming pools, called
lagares. Imagine happy people jumping about in bare feet,
squashing the grapes and singing along to a local band primed
to keep the momentum high. Doing the whole fermentation
and maturing of wines in concrete is a hugely fashionable
option since the advent of the concrete egg – an eye-wateringly
expensive, egg-shaped concrete tank that is being used in fine
winemaking everywhere from Bordeaux to New Zealand. The
egg-shape promotes natural movement through convection
currents as the wine ferments, so the wine is effectively being
gently stirred, giving the lees (yeast) more contact with the
wine. Like oak, concrete is porous and allows a gentle oxidative
development in the wines as they age. Unlike oak, concrete
doesn't impart any flavours to the wine. Eggs, therefore, tend
to produce rounder wines with a fuller texture.

Clay Amphora

These are the trendiest, modern winemaking vessels, no
question. Like sunglasses indoors, they provide instant 'cool' to
the owner, but everyone quietly suspects they're a pretentious
nob. They are also likely to be the oldest form of winemaking
vessel, with examples found in what is now the country of
Georgia from about 8,000 years ago. They have never gone
away, with regions such as the beautiful Alentejo in southeast
Portugal using clay pots called *talhas* for easily 2,000 years.
They are beautiful, fragile things (like the author) and are
eminently useful (unlike the author) as they impart no flavour
or aroma to the wine but, like concrete and granite, are a little
porous and allow oxygen to interact gently with the wine. Like
concrete eggs, the shape of the amphora also creates natural
movement within the wine as it ferments, stirring it gently and

building a richness of texture. In fact, the shape of the concrete egg is based on the amphora pot.

Winemakers choose the vessels they use for fermentation and maturation based on the style of wine they are aiming to achieve. It's very common for winemakers to transfer wine from one type of vessel to another at different stages – to get the best of both worlds. Fermenting a wine in oak, with the natural heat fermentation creates or draws more oak character from the barrel than transferring already-fermented wine into a barrel to rest and mature, for example. A winemaker may ferment in steel to benefit from the temperature control and retain lots of zingy fruit purity, then give that same wine some time in oak afterwards to broaden out and add further complexity.

Maturation in the Winery

This whole business of ageing wines after they have com-pleted fermentation falls under the term 'maturation'. You may hear about 'mature wines' in the context of old, classic vintages of a particular wine, or about wines being at their 'perfect maturity', the moment a wine of some potential is at its peak for drinking. Maturation is also every single moment a wine spends ageing post-fermentation, in whatever vessel that might be. It includes the years it hangs out in the bottle, too. Maturation starts as fermentation ends. Maturation ends the moment you twist
the cap or pierce the cork with an opener. What happens to the wine between those moments has as much impact on the wine you taste as any other part of the process.

While in the winery, any time spent in wood barrels has a distinct impact on the wine. Hearteningly, using oak isn't a linear or easily planned process. Common sense would lead you to expect a wine aged in oak to get more and more 'oaky' the longer it spends in the barrel. And it does work that way sometimes. Other times it seems not to.

Wines with barrel-age or other maturity have layers of character and texture rarely found in wines without maturity. They can demand a moment's fleeting attention and spark inspiration in even the most hardened non-interested wine drinker. There's no getting away from it, though, buying mature wine is a calculated lucky dip. It's hard to know exactly how the maturity will present in a specific wine at a specific moment in its life. That's the game . . . Consciously or not, you bring an understanding of how oak and maturation work on a wine. Bump this knowledge up against the available information on the wine label (grape variety, region and any details on oak ageing time, etc.) and you'll find yourself making a guestimate as to how it will have turned out. Sometimes the wine in the bottle follows the logic exactly, other times it may surprise you – you just have to embrace the potential.

Of course, you could reduce this exciting jeopardy by googling the hell out of the wine, seeking feedback from others who have opened the bottle before. Perhaps enlist the services of an influencer on social media (*Am I one of those? Probably. Yikes!*). Personally, I like the fun of exploring a wine only by pouring the first glass. Nosing about in it, swirling it raffishly, making the connections. I try to embrace the potential of something unexpected happening. In a world of commercialised food and drink, factory-achieved consistency in hermetically sealed containers, wine's rebellious, non-conformist ability to surprise and delight is something I want to celebrate and welcome.

Filtration (and Why Wines Are Not Always Vegan Friendly . . .)

Most wines require a bit of filtration before bottling. Some don't. Largely it depends on what the winemaker wishes to achieve and what the consumer expects. Filtration is used principally to remove particles clouding up the finished wine – these are mainly spent yeasts left over from fermentation, but also other particles that might have bound together at one stage or another.

Some wines are not filtered, whether for traditional reasons, or to be modern and very cool. Done well, it can give extra texture and character to the wine. Unfiltered wines sometimes sit a little cloudy in the bottle. Most wine consumers tend to expect clear wine. For this reason, unfiltered wines tend to be aimed at the more adventurous drinker.

Filtered or unfiltered, the wine may be anywhere on the scale from crap to extraordinary. It is no reflection on quality, only a stylistic choice. It's worth noting, you can drink the yeast. It ain't bad for ya.

The simplest form of filtration, if time is on the winemaker's side, is to let the particles settle at the bottom of the tank or barrel and then gently pump the wine above into a new vessel. It works well but takes a lot of time to achieve. So, to speed things up, winemakers often use something called 'fining agents' prior to filtration. These are usually liquid solutions dropped into the wine after the fermentation. In essence, they have a molecular-bonding ability, which attract and bind to the minute particles floating in the wine as they pass. Traditionally, ox blood (yes, blood) was used, but it hasn't been used for many decades. Nowadays, egg whites, isinglass (derived from fish), gelatine and bentonite clay are some of the common fining agents used. The fining agent is added in tiny quantities and remains separated from the wine, so is easily removed without trace afterwards.

Winemakers may choose to use a proper filter, too. These are good at removing larger particles. The key principle for all winemakers here is to be as gentle and minimalistic as possible. Overzealous filtration can affect aroma and flavour. Badly done, it can strip wines of their subtle nuances and rob them of their most unique characters. Most filtration moves the wine through a series of fine filters, often using natural diatomaceous earth (tiny, finely ground silica).

The interesting point to be made on filtration, I reckon, is that because it is so egregiously dull to think about, quite understandably very few wine drinkers ever give it much attention. Until quite recently, consumers didn't give much thought as to what agents or additives might be used. It turns out, it's quite a weird bunch and, crucially, many fining agents are derived from animals. Despite them being removed as part of the process and not being present in the final wine, their use would upset an unsuspecting vegan or vegetarian.

For this reason, some wines aren't suitable for all diets. Producers are getting better at identifying this on the bottle, but it isn't perfect. If you are vegan or vegetarian, I'd err on the side of caution. Call me a barefoot Brighton hippy (and many do), but I'm pro making as much wine as possible, animal product free. It's very easy. There are plenty of viable non-animal-derived fining agents available, like bentonite. Let everyone enjoy the party!

Bottling and Sulphites

Bottling wine, or filling other containers such as the bags in boxes or cans, completes the production journey. A multitude of dry goods (labels, bottles, corks, screw caps, etc.) come together to finish the job. The process tends to take place on a bottling line with empty glass bottles put on one end by hand, which is a hugely repetitive, high-tempo job, I can tell you from first-hand experience. Filled and closed bottles are labelled. Finally, they are packed by hand into wine boxes to protect them. Some wineries do this all themselves, many small- and medium-sized operations arrange for an external mobile bottling line on a lorry to arrive on a regular basis to process new stock.

As the wine is bottled, it's very common for a small quantity of sulphites to be added to the wine. This acts as an antioxidant and antimicrobial, protecting the wine as it ages. The quantities added vary dramatically from none to a maximum of 200mg per litre for some dry white wines in the EU. Reds get less, as they have much higher levels of natural antioxidants, tannin and other polyphenols. Sweet wines get more. To give it context, dried fruits, like apricots, can have up to 2,000mg of sulphites per kilogram of fruit. So, comparatively, the levels in wine are not enormous. Sulphites can be quite divisive. A small number of people (estimates suggest two per cent of the general population and up to fifteen per cent of asthmatics) experience negative reactions, typically wheezing and tight chest symptoms. Extreme reactions are thankfully very rare but do occur. If they have been added, the wine label will contain a clear warning that there are sulphites present. A tiny quantity of sulphur is naturally produced in the fermentation process, so sulphite-free wine is technically impossible without significant tinkering in a lab.

My position at present on sulphites is that they're often a necessary addition for wines built to age long periods. I think that certainly the lower the levels, the better. I am hugely interested in producers using other antioxidant techniques to allow them to use no or very few sulphites. The greater quantity of sugar in the wine, the higher the risk of microbial spoilage, hence the higher number of sulphites in sweet wines. Meanwhile, carbon dioxide and tannin are good natural protectants in wines, hence the lower number of sulphates often found in sparkling wines (carbon dioxide) and red wines (tannin).

Maturation in Bottle

Never is the non-linear process of maturation clearer than in the development of a wine once in the bottle. If you have the chance to taste anything within a few days or weeks of bottling, it is fascinating to realise that it is very rarely in its best state. These invasive moments (bottling still wines, disgorging sparkling wines) in a wine's lifetime shake up the cool, calm and collected vision the wine is hoping to portray and exposes the fragile, limpid parts one-by-one. Wait a while on any new vintage, is my suggestion – even fresh, zippy, drink-'em-young wine styles, like Provence rosé or New Zealand Sauvignon Blanc, benefit from a month or two in a bottle. Plus, when it comes to transportation, all that shaking and lifting and activity often causes wines to close up and hide their finest details. Give wines a little time to settle.

Development of more flavour, texture and broader aromas (maturation in the bottle) comes from the gentle ingress of oxygen through the porous cork or breathable screw cap. That constant low-level hum of oxygen gently buffs the fresh edges of the wine in the bottle, tickles the fruity, aromatic notes into evolution and adds subtle, nutty character to the wine. Oaky, savoury character and some rich fruit elements of a wine often get more expressive over time in bottle, the oxygen bringing them more and more to the fore. A wine's colour also changes as it matures. Oxygen slowly deepens white wine's colour to a honey yellow, even amber hue. Reds lose a little pigmentation, which forms the sediment you often find in old red wine bottles. Reds lose their colour as they age, therefore, turning slowly more brick red and translucent. This takes an enormous amount of time. Wines with months or even a few years of maturity in bottle may not look very different to when they were first bottled.

Slow as it may be, as in life, the maturation process glides steadily forwards taking each individual wine on a unique journey with highs and lows along the way. Wine ages in peaks and troughs. The same wine may be delicious on release but have heavy bitter tannins or astringent acidity that make it challenging to enjoy. As the wine ages in bottle, there will be moments where the fruit characters, those tannins and the acidity, reach a moment of complete harmony. Then, years or months later, they may fall out of balance again, only to re-harmonise in a new equilibrium further down the track. It's all subjective; one person's perfectly balanced Bordeaux is another's mahogany and leather-tinged nightmare. Each to their own – the trick is to try to open the bottle when it's in a good spot for you. The only way to do this, really, is to buy a case or two and open bottles as the wine ages, tasting and making judgements on where each component of the wine is at that moment; guessing where they are heading and when they'll be in song together. Great fun, but a complete frivolity and not something accessible to many.

Luckily, you can buy already-bottle-mature wines. Fully matured wines sell at a price premium, as they have been carefully stored over the years and left to reach their 'peak potential'. They are, by their nature, rare, as most of their siblings were opened and drunk many years previously. Crucially, mature wines are highly priced because buying them from a good merchant who knows their stuff takes a large amount of the risk out of drinking older wines. You could very easily have the same experience for a snip of the price, had you chosen the right wine to age in the first place, bought it when it was first released, then waited patiently, caring for it for all that time, waiting to find the perfect moment in its evolution to crack it open. Some stuff under my stairs looked great in theory, but half a decade later it isn't quite as interesting as I thought it would be . . .

Most of that hairy business is alleviated when buying mature wines that are ready to drink. Someone else has borne the tedium; so, for a premium, you can just tuck in. That is not to say that there is 'no risk' to buying mature wines in shops. Like second-hand cars, etiquette tends to be that you buy them 'as seen', understanding and accepting they may be incredible, or indeed may not be. There may be a fault to them, imperceptible until opened, or they may just be knackered.

There are no refunds. It is an inherent part of the mature wine thing. A calculated roll of the dice.

Side note: it is different in restaurants. Etiquette dictates that you may refuse a bottle if you think it's corked or faulty in any way. That's why you may be offered to smell the wine before it is served to the table. Don't worry about doing this, if you feel the wine is genuinely faulty, as the restaurant recoups the cost of the bottle from their supplier, who in turn recoups from the producer. You are not being a dick. If the wine is fine and you just don't 'like' it . . . then you have to drink it, or you are being a dick.

Sparkling Wine

Sparkling wine production follows the rhythms of still winemaking but with some specific extra moments in the journey. There are a number of ways to produce sparkling wine, the most common being the Traditional Method (used in Champagne, Cava, English and many other sparkling wines), Charmat Method (Prosecco and some others), Pet Nat and other 'natural' bottle-fermented fizz, and simple carbonation. To make a wine sparkling, winemakers must capture carbon dioxide in the wine, forming bubbles. Fermentations create carbon dioxide alongside alcohol, so most methods involve retaining this naturally produced carbon dioxide within the wine. However, often sparkling wine producers create dozens of individual still wines from different plots of land before this carbon-dioxide-capturing stage, each with their own unique character, then blend them together. With careful consideration, this blending allows the producer to create a consistent style year-on-year.

Carbonation is the only method that adds carbon dioxide from another source into the wine. Let's knock this one on the head swiftly. You can carbonate a still wine to make it fizzy. It's relatively rare that this is done to bottled sparkling wines, but very common in canned sparkling wines; anything still from a can feels a bit flat, so a light carbonation is common. In the quality spectrum of fizz, carbonation is pretty low . . . It's cheap, quick and easy. You won't encounter this much so we won't dwell on it here.

Traditional Method

Traditional Method sparkling is the top-tier, proper-fancy, no-corners-cut method. It is the internationally recognised name for this production process. You will also see it written as *méthode champenoise* in France (protected for use only by Champagne). Champagne can lay claim to the development and refinement of this method over centuries. Notably, though, the first documented use of the method was actually in England in 1662. A chap called Christopher Merrett wrote about imported wines having raisins added to them to force a second fermentation and provide some bubbles. There is good evidence that a similar idea had caught on much earlier in cider-making in England, too . . . So, England proudly holds the claim to the first spark of inspiration, at least forty years prior to the French.

Traditional Method wines are commonly made in cool-climate regions, as to find the right balance in the final product they really require high acidity (to allow ageing and keep them refreshing) and low alcohol in the base wine (10.5–11 per cent). Warmer regions do make this style of wine, but to achieve it they usually use fruit picked earlier in the season and from higher altitudes, where you find the cooler plots of land.

The prepared still wine has a little more yeast and sugar added to it, known as the tirage. This kicks off a second fermentation. But, before the second fermentation begins, the wine (now gently cloudy with yeast) is put into a bottle and closed with a crown cap. This closes off the inside of the bottle to the outside world, making it totally sealed and inert.

The bottle is laid on its side in a cool, pitch-black place, such as a cellar. Over the coming weeks, the second fermentation slowly takes place in the bottle. Yeasts consume the sugars and produce carbon dioxide and alcohol. The carbon dioxide cannot escape from the bottle, so it dissolves into the liquid in the form of bubbles. As the pressure inside the bottle grows (often reaching 6 bars by the end), the bubbles get tighter and more miniscule and firm in their attack. The second fermentation will have brought the final alcohol level in the wine up to around 12 per cent ABV (alcohol by volume).

Once the yeasts (lees) have consumed the available sugars, they cease activity and become dormant. At this time, they sink and lie along the full length of the side of the bottle. Over time, the yeast begins to impart new texture, aroma and flavour to the wine. It starts very slowly, building a little richness. Gradually, subtle toasty, pastry, biscuity notes begin to develop. The longer a Traditional Method wine is aged on the lees, the more these new characters take hold over the fresh, citrussy, fruity character from the grapes themselves. If you want to be geeky, this process is called autolysis and the toasty characters it imparts can be described as 'autolytic character'. Stick that in your lexicon, you massive boff.

The winemaker has control over exactly when they think the perfect balance of yeasty character has been achieved. A year or two may give a little extra complexity and texture to a fruit-driven, fresh-styled wine. Many years more can achieve enormously rich, deep, powerfully flavoured wines with less pure fruit. In many ways, wines ageing in this state are in a time capsule – nothing is getting in, nothing is getting out. In the right environment, the greatest wines can age for many decades in this state, just getting more and more complex.

When it is time, the winemaker must remove the lees from the bottle. To do this they gently turn the bottle, agitating the yeast inside with every minute movement, and tip the bottle up until it is completely upside-down. The lees slide into the neck of the bottle, coming to rest on the crown cap and forming a little layer of yeast about a centimetre deep. This process of gently turning the bottle is known as 'riddling'. The upside-down bottle is then dipped, about an inch deep, in a highly chilled liquid bath. This freezes a solid plug of ice at the top of the bottle, trapping all the yeast sediment within it. Then, the crown cap is removed from the bottle and the pressure inside from the natural carbon dioxide fires the plug of ice out of the bottle. If nicely cool, the rest of the bottle's contents remain calmly in the bottle, much like when you pull a cork from a bottle at home. This process to remove the crown cap and yeast is called disgorging or *dégorgement*.

The bottle is then topped up with more of the same wine, and usually a little sulphur and sugar is added. The sugar helps balance the wine and is known as the dosage. The average quantity added would be somewhere between eight and twelve grams per litre for a dry (brut) sparkling wine. Less dosage makes the wine more tart, and more gives a sensation of fullness. You'll find both if you look for them, from zero to very high levels of sugar. To make Traditional Method wines taste noticeably quite sweet, it would typically take around thirty-two grams per litre, which is what the *Champenois* would call 'demi-sec'.

Once the dosage is added (or isn't), a cork is pushed into the bottle and a muselet (wire cage) added to secure the cork. Done. Like all wines, a period of time ageing in the bottle to let the wine settle is beneficial, and this is even more so the case with Traditional Method sparkling. Ideally, I like to have at least six months bottle age before tucking in.

You are in no urgency to drink most Traditional Method sparkling wines. As they age in bottle, sparkling wines develop gentle nuttiness and sometimes subtle burnt-caramel aromas. They also slowly lose their fizz over decades, as the carbon dioxide bubbles bind together and get larger and less aggressive. So, again, it's just down to what you want in your sparkling . . . I like a bit of both!

Charmat Method

The Charmat Method is a little simpler than the Traditional Method. It's also much quicker, which results in winemakers being able to sell the wine more swiftly and at a lower price, as they don't bear the costs of storing wine for years before release. It is, therefore, usually used to produce sparkling wines that are intentionally fruit-focussed and available at lower price points, such as Prosecco. While it doesn't allow for the complexity and age-ability of wines made in the Traditional Method, it isn't an inferior process, just stylistically different.

As before, it starts with still wines at relatively low alcohol (10.5–11.5 per cent) in a tank. These still wines have a tirage of new sugar and yeast added, which kicks off a second fermentation. Where the Charmat Method deviates is during this second fermentation, which takes place inside the tank, not in the bottle. A special (and very expensive) pressurised tank holds the wine during its second fermentation, closed completely to retain all the carbon dioxide released by the fermentation. This carbon dioxide dissolves into the wine as the pressure builds inside the tank, forming bubbles. Once fermentation is complete, the wine is fully fizzy and ready to go. Some wines may be aged in the tank in contact with the lees for a few days or months to give a little extra richness and texture, many are not.

The fully fizzy wine is filtered and bottled under pressure, direct from the tank. As the wine goes into the bottle, the bubbles are bumped about a bit and the process tends to create larger, softer-feeling bubbles as a result. The overall pressure inside the bottles tends to be lower than those of Traditional Method sparkling, too. For this reason, Charmat Method wines have an easy drinkability to them that is hugely attractive.

Charmat wines tend not to age as well as Traditional Methods, though. They are typically styles to drink within a year or so of production. This is partly due to the method and the less-firm carbon dioxide structure, but more about the character of the grapes used. Charmat grapes are usually riper, fruitier and more aromatic. The production method can celebrate and highlight these characters, without adding more character, as the Traditional Method would, so they are best enjoyed while those bright, aromatic notes are fresh.

Pet Nat

In many ways, this is the original sparkling wine. Winemakers have been making semi-fizzy, cloudy wines since day one, usually by accident. In fact, the man himself, Dom Perignon of Champagne fame, dedicated much of his winemaking life in the late 1600s and early 1700s to working out why their carefully created still wines that tasted so nice at Christmas kept going a little bit fizzy the following spring. It drove him wild! Let me explain . . .

Pet Nat is a buzzy shortening of the French term *Pétillant Naturel*. Lightly fizzy (*pétillant*) wines are produced naturally by bottling the wine before it has finished its first fermentation. The wine goes into bottle with some alcohol, lots of yeast and a fair amount of natural sugar still present. Once in the bottle, a crown cap secures the environment and the fermentation completes within the closed space. Like the Traditional Method, this creates bubbles, albeit usually at a lower pressure (3 bar, maybe).

Once the fermentation is finished, the wine is sold as it is. The crown cap is the stopper, rather than popping the bottle open and adding a cork. This leaves the yeasts inside and, crucially, doesn't allow winemakers to add sugar to season, as they do in the Traditional Method. Pet Nats tend to be bone dry, as the yeasts have consumed all available sugar in the ferment.

Pet Nats are a rustic, fun style of wine usually consumed within the year of production. It is at the consumer's discretion whether they want to shake the bottle gently to mix the yeasts into the wine (which makes it go a bit cloudy) or pour the wine gently so the first few glasses are clear of yeast; it gets more cloudy as you drink through the bottle. The yeasts add richness and texture to the palate, which can be nice in lieu of long ageing or sugar to broaden the wine.

There are variations on the Pet Nat process the world over. In Italy, a similar style called Col Fondo is popular and the method is used around the world today. Col Fondo is the original Prosecco in many ways; how it was done before the late 1800s invention of the pressurised tanks used today. Col Fondo translates as 'with the bottom' . . . i.e. bottled with the yeasts left to sit at the bottom of the bottle. Col Fondo differs to Pet Nat in that the base wine is fully fermented, then a tirage of new yeast and sugar is added just before bottling, so there is a second fermentation in the bottle, rather than just the first fermentation finishing in the bottle. It allows more control over the final wine's exact fizz. Col Fondo wines are not disgorged either, so tend to be sold with a crown cap closure and the yeast still inside, as with Pet Nat.

Sweet and Fortified Wine

In a more health-conscious world where alcoholic units and sugars are measured gram by embarrassing gram, sweet wines certainly have a hurdle to overcome. Hugely popular historically, the international wine palate seems to be getting drier and drier, so sales of these majestic beasts are in decline.

Sweet wines are largely made in the same way as still wines. They are often oak-aged to add richness, spice and weight. The key thing is that they are produced from grapes that achieve high levels of ripeness (high sugar levels) and the fermentation doesn't consume them all; it ends before the yeasts have finished the job. This might be because a winemaker intervenes; quickly chilling the wine renders yeasts inactive and they can then be filtered out to stop the fermentation permanently. Grapes may be dried after picking to reduce water and concentrate sugars before pressing. It might also be a natural thing. Botrytis, a particular type of rot, dehydrates grapes on the vine and creates incredibly complex flavours. In these high-sugar situations, the yeasts can struggle to do their work; fermentations can take many months, even years in some cases. Sometimes the yeasts might struggle to ferment all of the sugar before the resulting booze gets too high (circa 15 per cent ABV for most yeast strains) and they die, leaving the remaining sugar in place.

Sweet wines, counter-intuitively, require enormous amounts of acidity alongside the sugar levels. Without acidity, they taste sickly and cloying. The finest German Rieslings, French Sauternes or Hungarian Tokaji all have a balancing, clean acidity that keeps them refreshing and moreish. The combination of sugar, acidity and intensity of flavour allows these wines to age for decades in the bottle.

Fortified wine is a broad category, taking in everything from Spain's sherry and Portugal's Port to lesser-considered gems like France's red Banyuls and Australia's Rutherglen Muscats. They can be bone-dry (Fino sherry), a little sweet, or the sweetest wines in the world. What they share is that, to a greater or lesser extent, there has been an addition of high-strength, distilled alcohol to the wine. This brings the alcohol content up sharply, often between 17 and 20 per cent ABV, and immediately ceases the fermentation.

Fortified winemakers often use spirit addition to retain lots of sweetness and 'fresh grape' character in a wine. For example, with the great sweet wines of Muscat de Setúbal in Portugal, the fermentation might only last for a couple of days before they fortify the wine with a 96 per cent ABV grape-based spirit to retain the Muscat's natural, aromatic, floral, juicy character. The vast majority of the final wine's alcohol comes from the spirit added, not the grape's fermented juice.

Fortified wines were mostly invented to allow wine to be transported around the world. The higher level of alcohol and sugar protected (fortified!) the wines on long journeys by ship across the seas. Today, this same benefit also helps their ability to age in the bottle. Most wines, once opened, need to be drunk quite swiftly, but fortified wines will last a week or so longer than most still wines. Some, especially Madeira, are bullet-proof and can last for many months after opening.

Natural Wine

A relatively recent, genuinely important and achingly cool phenomenon within the industry, the term 'natural wine' covers a diverse bunch of wines and winemakers providing a counter-culture to the highly visible, commercial, big brand wines we see every day. 'Natural' is not an official certification, more a loose international category of wines that share a broad ethos.

This shared ethos tends to mean a more transparent, minimalistic approach to their production processes. They completely remove, or at least heavily reduce, the more invasive processes and additives common in modern wine-making. Commercially sensible sulphur additions, added sugar, commercial yeasts, winemaking chemicals for fining – get out! The wines are often organic or biodynamic. Really, we're talking the closest thing possible to squashed and fermented grapes put in a bottle. Un-masked, unadulterated, minimal tickling and polishing.

In this respect, despite being a 'modern' trend, natural wines are often made with traditional methods first used centuries ago. The natural wine movement has been brilliant at shining a fresh spotlight on wine styles dating back 8,000 years or more and bringing them to wider attention, for example, orange wine aged in amphora has been alive and well, without pause for centuries, in countries like Georgia and in quiet pockets of otherwise well-known wine regions, like Italy's Collio on the Slovenian–Italian border. In every winemaking country in the world, these practices are now being experimented with to produce orange wines.

While there have been producers and consumers championing the equivalent of natural wines since the 1960s and way before, the movement gained increasing attention through the 2000s and 2010s, and in the last ten years has become an indisputably important segment of the wine world. Producers in French regions like the Loire and Beaujolais were pivotal in bringing high-quality, critically acclaimed, low-intervention natural wines to the fore. Today, natural wines are made everywhere, in every style.

In its keenness to step away from the staid, traditional wine scene, natural wine has been a major contributor to modern wine labelling using brighter, cleaner, more fun design and brand messaging. With it, natural wine has contributed enormously to attracting a new generation of wine drinkers.

The diversity and looseness of natural wine is both its greatest asset and its greatest barrier as a category. With no clear rules to follow or standardised level of quality, it isn't really a category at all. Many producers considered 'natural' by consumers don't think of themselves as natural. With no set of prescribed natural wine requirements and no certification body guarding the term's use on a label, they worry it is a term ripe for misuse by less scrupulous marketeers. As such, natural wines have provided wine drinkers with a wider, more experiential range of wines to readily explore, but can sometimes be a bit hit and miss when it comes to what to expect from the wines themselves.

Here are some well-known 'natural' producers to start you off: Testalonga (South Africa); Mas de Daumas Gassac (France); Cramele Recaş (Romania); and Pheasant's Tears (Georgia).

3.

How to Taste Wine

There is a wealth of information written about wine-tasting technique. I think, like with table manners or social etiquette, it's good to know 'the done thing'. It's also important to know when to apply that knowledge and when to let it slide. Technical wine-tasting has its place and in many ways is hugely beneficial to anyone wanting to enjoy wine more. Like anything, though, it can be used to exclude those who haven't been trained in it and, historically, I think a lot of people felt a little like wine was something for other people, not them. This was in part because they didn't know the lingo and were worried about the correct way to hold a glass. There's no reason why you should know. Once you do, it's easy and it'll help you get more from your wine.

That said, however you choose to deliver wine into your senses is fine with me. As long as you feel you're getting the most out of it, then be my guest. I'd rather you poured it in to a shallow tray and lapped at it with your tongue, than you swirled a crystal glass obnoxiously and tried to make fun of how other people do it.

So, let's look at the 'proper' way to taste wine and then, knowing this, you can build in the nuance that makes you feel comfy around it.

The Technique

The Palate

First and foremost, it's all about your nose. It's perfect. It's also enormously sensitive to the subtle nuances and unique aromas of whatever you put in front of it. Initially, when you consciously try to smell wine the first few times, it does, as many people say, just smell like wine. That's entirely correct. Then, when you've sniffed about a bit, you'll notice that one wine has a more citrussy kind of smell – ish – and that the one over there makes you think about pineapples a bit more. Before you know it, if you keep giving wine a sniff, consciously or not, you'll build a frame of reference for the stuff. You'll soon get a kind of par average in mind for how strongly wines smell, how sweet they taste, etc. and you'll begin to know where on the spectrum the wine in your glass right now falls.

The nose being such a good tool to assess a wine's unique aromatic character means professionals spend a fair amount of time sniffing at glasses. Once you put the wine in your mouth, the aromas rise through the oral cavity at the back of your mouth and return to tickling your olfactory senses in your nose, giving a perception of taste. The tongue itself is great at picking up acidity levels, bitterness and sweetness. So, you can gauge these elements of a wine only when you swirl it about in your mouth a bit.

People worry enormously that they don't have a 'good palate'. I think this is understandable. I also think it is total nonsense. Like anything else in the human body, one's palate is constantly in flux. Your age, your energy levels, your sleep cycles, your diet, your current environment, the time of day, your emotion, you name it, it all effects your perception of aroma and taste at any given moment. The idea of great tasters and rubbish tasters isn't down to biology, it's down to personal calibration. Forget everyone else, just get to know you. Your palate is unique and moves with you wherever you go and whatever you are feeling.

Understand how things taste to you, what elements of aroma and flavour you are more sensitive to and which bits you have to focus on more. Most importantly, try not to be swayed by others' opinions. If your pal says the wine tastes like oranges and blossom, and you think it's a grapefruit peel and white pepper situation, you're both correct; there is no right and wrong here. Every palate is valid. Everyone can taste wine. It's just a case of tasting as much as possible to build up the bank of experience.

Sight

The wine glass is designed for you to stick your nose in and have a good sniff. It also allows you to swirl wine round inside, which is both fun and beneficial. Swirling releases aromas into the bowl of the wine glass, which are then more readily available for you to find. Swirling is part and parcel of wine tasting. It can feel a bit awkward or clunky at first but keep practising and it becomes second nature. I absentmindedly swirl cups of tea and glasses of water now . . . which I think adds to my flamboyant character. Others probably just think I'm a tit.

Before swirling, you want to take a quick look at the colour of the wine. It doesn't tell you much, but it can be a good initial lead. Lighter whites tend to be youthful and unaged; the more golden and amber, the more likelihood they have been oak aged or matured in the bottle. Reds, too. Bright ruby colours lead you towards younger red wines; subtle orangey, paler rims around the edges of the glass might lead you towards more mature, older wines.

And the translucency is definitely a thing to consider. Can you see through the wine? Almost all whites you can, for sure, but consider how water-clear it is. Reds can range from being totally translucent and pale, through to ink black and opaque. More translucent, paler wine will tend to either be older and aged, or a more gently pressed, less extractive style, which would suggest lighter tannins and a fresher wine. But, as with all things in wine, there are exceptions. You'll have to taste it and see if your assumptions are correct.

Oh, and as for 'the legs' (how the wine clings to the walls of the glass after swirling), these have been wildly over focussed on in films and popular culture. Higher sugar levels make them fall slower, higher alcohol more quickly. As such, you get a mish-mash of combined information by studying them... just ignore.

Smell

Swirl away. Get your nose in the glass and take relaxed, calm sniffs. Some people do lots of little sniffs, some people take longer, drawn-out ones; do what feels right for you. Try to consider how intense the aromas are. Does it leap out at you, or is it quite subtle? Give it a moment and return for another sniff. Your nose gets tired quite quickly when sniffing alcohol, so take it at a leisurely pace. Don't try to force ideas around specific aromas into your head, try to just let your memory recall where you smelt that sort of thing before. You'll come up with few ideas at first, then, the more you taste, the more you'll recognise the details in there.

Some key things to consider might be: is it citrussy? Is it opulent ripe fruits or more restrained? Is it spicy, earthy, savoury? Are they fresh fruits, dried, or cooked in some way? Is there a herby or waxy note? Are there lots of aromas mingling together or just one or two? The list could go on and on. You'll find your way through and a way that works for you. Many people have a set order of things they consider when tasting, they analytically move through the process. They're probably better than me, but I like to swirl and sniff with as calm and blank a mind as possible and let the characters find me. I work on the basis that if it's there, it'll show itself to me if I'm relaxed. The wine will dictate the order in which I notice its elements. Do what works for you.

Taste

Once you decide to have a sip, you should ideally have already built up a picture of the wine's character from the sight and the nose. Sip and hold the wine in your mouth, let it roll around a bit and touch all the corners of your tongue. Your tongue picks up key senses like sweetness, acidity and bitterness in different places, so touching them all is key. Some people make a horrible slurping noise at this point, drawing air in through their mouth over the wine. It opens the wine up a bit, is the theory, and helps bring out its unique character. It probably helps a bit but at the expense of everyone within earshot wanting to smother you with the tablecloth. I confess, I sometimes make that noise. My wife Olivia can't stand it.

Think, as you continue to swirl. How much is my mouth watering? This will tell you the acidity level. What is the texture I am sensing? Is it thick and viscous, like milk, or thin like water? Is it grippy on my cheeks? How grippy? Soft, chewy grippy, or dry, harsh grippy? How intense are the flavours? How warm does the alcohol feel?

Spit or swallow. Come on, you're better than that. Now's the time to consider the length in your mouth. How long do the flavours linger? Is it the full spectrum of flavours in the wine, or do the bitter or acidic or sweet notes outlast the others? Great wine at all price points has total balance – long, lingering flavours, each in harmony, long after you have swallowed.

Taste wine consciously, regularly enough and you'll build up that brilliant frame of reference. You'll get dialled in tightly on how much alcohol is in a wine, just by how concentrated the mouthfeel is and how warm the sensation. You'll know a wine has low acidity within seconds of it hitting your palate, as your mouth waters less than before. You'll recognise the wine in your glass is a carnival of fruit-salad flavour compared to most. It will just be there. Taste as much as possible, as often as possible.

The other, often overlooked, thing that will help your wine tasting is having a rich and diverse catalogue of what stuff smells like in your head. Having direct experience of the spectrum of sensations available to the human nose and tongue outside of wine will give you the range of descriptors required to articulate wine effectively. That menthol and herbaceous twang, bitter-sweet combinations, that magic when salt, acid and fat meet; be conscious of your hedonistic experience as often as possible. I have friends in the wine trade that sniff EVERYTHING. They can't walk past a window box without stopping. Bugger that. But, if you get a chance to be conscious and enjoy aroma and flavour, then take it. It will help.

Wine Pulled Apart – Key Components and What Makes 'Good' or 'Bad' Wine

Outside of the nuts and bolts we've talked about, everyone has their own way to process the information gleaned when tasting wine. How you mentally categorise wines is entirely up to you. I think about wines in terms of shapes and as having 'energy'. The shapes thing is common among professionals. Tensely acidic, clean, fruity wines feel sharp and angular, whereas lower acids feel smoother edged and ripe fruits feel soft and round. Rich, creamy texture alongside concentrated fruit flavour feels 'enormous'. Tannins add lots of weight and give a square, bulky sensation. So, I'll often describe a wine as linear or straight-lined, or 'huge' or round. Once you get into it, it really begins to make sense, but it's definitely one of those things that can feel a bit ridiculous or inaccessible on starting out. 'What does that awful guy mean when he says this Albariño is statuesque?!'

The energy thing is less common, but helps me make sense of wine. Zippy acid and crunchy, fresh fruits are uplifting and high-toned elements that, to me, make a wine feel high energy. A creamy-textured, soft, plummily fruited, gently chewy, woody-spiced red feels low energy, mellow stuff to me. That's the idea. It isn't a conscious thing; it's a subconscious characterisation. Much like when you listen to music; it evokes a sensation of energy.

So, what are these sensations? What should we be keeping an eye out for when tasting? Good question. Here's how they typically present themselves:

Acidity

Only really discoverable on the palate, acidity can be hinted at on the nose, too. Acidity tends to walk hand-in-hand with the ripeness of grapes. So, if you smell a wine that has lower ripeness and cool climate characteristics (tense lemon or lime citrus, fresh green apple, that sort of thing) then your brain will automatically begin to expect some fresh acidity.

On the palate, acidity feels like a little electric zing, a tension. It is fine structured and lively. It makes your mouth water. The degree to which you get these sensations will indicate the level of acidity.

Acidity is masked on the palate by sugar. So, sweet wines often have much more acidity than you might think. Bear that in mind when tasting sweeter, riper wines. Is your mouth still watering? Do they feel oddly refreshing and not too cloying? Acid.

There are a range of acids that you taste in wine. The three key acids occurring naturally are malic, tartaric and lactic. Each gives a subtly different sensation. Malic is super-fresh and cutting in its approach, like fresh apples straight from the tree. Tartaric acid is slightly salty and very citrussy. Lactic is more creamy and rich; a softer, more mouth-filling acidity. Depending on the balance between these acids, wine will appear more tart or creamy.

While these occur naturally, winemakers can add acid to a wine if they want to. That said, additions of acid are banned in the majority of wine region legislations, the only exceptions being where it is very hot indeed. It isn't a celebrated thing; winemakers should really be picking grapes while they have the right acid level. So, it's rare to find added acidity in premium wine. Tartaric is the most commonly added acid, though sometimes it is citric. These can stabilise and balance the wine but, if not treated very carefully, they can leave a tangy, sharp sensation that sits outside the harmony of the rest of the wine.

Sweetness

Again, only discoverable on the palate, although you can gain strong hints that a wine will be sweet from the nose. Sweetness comes from ripe, sweet grapes, so 'ripe' aromas of dried apricots, figs, damson and honey will get your head thinking 'sweet' when you smell them.

You know the sensation of sweetness. We all adore it. Our tastebuds sing, our bodies get that little lifting sensation, that gentle buzz of anticipation and joy. The key thing with sweetness in wine is that it must be in balance with refreshing acidity to keep it limber and avoid a sticky, cloying sensation. Acidity pushes back against sweetness, so high-acid wines with lots of sweetness will feel both less acidic and less sweet than would otherwise be the case. Mosel Riesling is a perfect example of this – rolling natural sweetness, but rapier-sharp and fresh as an outdoor shower.

Tannin

Harder to anticipate from the nose than acidity or sweetness, tannin is a palate-only sensation. Tannin binds to protein molecules, like your cheeks and gums. It gives a grippy, drying sensation. It can exist in tiny quantities in white and rosé wines, through to very high quantities in some reds and orange wines. It comes from grape skins, stems and a little from oak barrels, so is most commonly found in reds.

At its lowest levels, it adds a sense of texture, ruggedness and weight to a wine. The tannin spectrum runs from a subtle cheek-drying, chalky sensation, through chewy and mouth-filling, to a bitter-coffee-powered, vice-like grip on your jaw.

Tannin level aside, tannins themselves come in a range of sensations. Ripe tannins from well-sunned vines appear more chewy, slightly softer, less astringent than lower-ripeness tannins, which can be quite sappy, aggressive and bitter.

Tannins from oak barrels have a softer, dry sensation. Grape
stalks can give 'green', astringent, sappy tannin. A little of each
is great; too much of any can overpower and unbalance.

As wines age, their tannic sensation reduces and softens.
The greatest long-lived wines, say First Growth Bordeaux
reds, are so tannic in their youth that you would never be able
to drink them joyfully. Tannins give wine the protection and
structure to age well. At a certain moment, whether a year or
a decade later, those once-harsh, liquorice and espresso-bean
monsters will yield just enough and the wine will find harmony.

Concentration

Simply, concentration refers to how flavourful and tightly
packed the wine is. You know a concentrated wine when you
taste it. Poor-quality wine can be a little watery, like pale tea or
too little cordial in your beaker. Low-concentration wines give
a bit of fruit flavour, a sensation of some kind of sweetness,
maybe a tense acidity, but they fall short of having the depth of
flavour at their core to hold it all together.

Well-concentrated wines start with a character, then drive
that character home through the mid-palate and on to a long,
clear finish after swallowing. At their best, they introduce new
aroma and flavour as you go along that journey, revealing
layers of fruit, minerals, aromatic herbs or other complexities,
wrapping them in a tight bouquet. This isn't about style of
wine. Concentrated wines can be subtle, elegant, refined or
wild and outlandishly flavourful and everything in between.
Concentrated wines have sensations of structure and depth on
the palate, even if it's within a tiny, little, elegant frame. They
harbour a powerful energy. Confident and honest, they are fine,
complete things, greater than the sum of their parts.

Fruit Quality

To a large extent, what defines good acidity, tannin and concentration in a wine is the quality of the grapes used to make it. Quality grapes harvested at peak ripeness, when enough acidity is retained, the tannins are ripe enough and the sugar levels are where they need to be, are hard won. It takes a fair bit of luck with a good vintage and careful observation from the winemaker. When tasting wine, you can tell high-quality fruit by the purity and definition of the fruit flavours. The cleanliness of them, the complex layers of character held together as one.

It's a hard thing to gauge initially, but the difference in lower-quality and higher-quality fruit becomes very clear with a bit of tasting experience. There is a lack of definition in lower-quality fruit's flavour; rather than being precise and characterful, they are more of a muddle of broad-brush, generic, mixed-fruit flavours. Think of the difference between out-of-season, generic strawberries and peak-season, Wimbledon-final strawberries. That's what I'm getting at.

Alcohol

Alcohol, specifically ethanol, plays a key role in our perception of the weight and intensity of a wine. Higher-alcohol wines invariably have more flavour and feel fuller, richer, heavier on the palate. This is partly because ethanol itself gives a viscous, full-bodied sensation. But also, the presence of higher alcohol usually means the wine is made from riper grapes, which are typically more flavourful. Conversely, lower-alcohol wines will have a sensation of lightness to them.

Ethanol has a flavour of its own, described as subtly fruity by many, and it adds a sensation of sweetness or gently oily bitterness to the drink, depending on the subjective palate of the taster. Alcohol is also a fantastic carrier of aroma and flavour, so higher-alcohol wines will often have increased perfume and aromatic lift to them when you sniff the glass. It gives a warming sensation, both on the nose and palate, which in the concentrations typically found in wines is relatively subtle, unlike when sniffing neat spirits, which takes a bit of getting used to! In great wines, the alcohol should feel well integrated, balanced, rather than being too noticeable.

Structure

All these key components of a wine combine to form a sensation of structure. This goes back to that tasting in shapes thing. It may be that a wine's structure is quite round and soft, it may be the opposite, firm and tense. One component, or more likely a combination of, the wine's acidity, alcohol, tannin and flavour will dictate its structure.

As you taste wine, you will be consciously aware of the wine's structure. Great wines feel well held together; they have a key component (often acidity or tannin) holding all the other elements in place. Less-good wines lack this structure; they can feel a bit disjointed, less harmonious, with the various components of flavour, sweetness, acidity and alcohol all pulling in different directions. Structure is a bit of a nebulous concept, but as you taste a broad range of wines, you'll find it makes sense!

Age-ability

A wine's ability to age is defined by a combination of its concentration, its structural components and its fruit quality. Acidity, alcohol, sweetness and tannin all help a wine remain in great shape over years tucked away in the bottle.

Wines built to age should really be a challenge to drink young. Fewer and fewer wines are made to be aged these days, though, driven by consumer demand for immediately accessible bottles. I am told that eighty-five per cent of wine is drunk within forty-eight hours of purchase, which says it all. We want wine and we want it now, or at least we want it for that barbecue at the weekend. Winemakers employ techniques like ageing in concrete tanks or barrels to soften the wines down, buff their sharp edges and make them accessible younger; fast-tracking what would have happened in bottle over a decade down to a year or so in the winery before release.

Every now and again, though, you will find a wine with super concentration and fine fruit that tastes great now, but is just a bit tight and tense. That wine might just benefit from a little time in bottle to broaden out. Similarly, those wines with aggressive tannins coming at your throat or bracing acidity that feels like it's going to hold firm for years to come, are those you can stick away. Even better if it has a combination of all these characteristics.

If you do decide to let it age, do it somewhere with a cool temperature, out of sunlight. A cellar with a consistent temperature is ideal but a rare thing, plus I'm scared of the dark, so I don't need that anxiety in my life. Under the stairs, away from radiators is my spot.

Balance

The sum of it all. Balance. Fickle, nebulous, absolute. The target and aspiration for every winemaker ever.

Perfect balance is a harmonious bouquet of aroma, flavour and textures, held together with good structure. No one element overshadowing the other or competing for space. Nothing sticking out. Nothing clunkily jammed in. A perfect journey from pour, to sniff, to sip, to finish.

Wines go in and out of perfect balance over their lifetime. Ageing through peaks and troughs.

Balance is a spectrum; it doesn't have to be perfect. Close to perfect balance is an extraordinary thing, too. Often the best food wines have near-perfect balance on their own, but with a nudge from the right food, fall perfectly into place.

4.

Drinking Etiquette and Stuff Worth Knowing

As with tasting technique, I think it's worth knowing the common etiquette and theatre around the drinking and serving of wine. Whether you choose to adopt this is entirely up to you. Let this be a quick reference guide of the stuff worth knowing and why it's done.

How to Hold a Wine Glass

There are specific glass shapes for specific wine styles. The classic, long, thin flute for Champagne, the round, bowl-shaped glass for white and red wine, the red often being larger than the white, etc. These work well for serving wine at a party. For tasting wine, when you want to get the most from the wine, everything should go in a regular, round, bowl-shaped wine glass. I tend to use a white wine glass with as thin a lip as possible.

It sounds silly, but there is an etiquette to holding your wine glass. It is simple: hold the stem, not the bowl. There. Done. The reason for this is that holding the bowl brings your hands close to the wine itself, the thin glass will warm up quite swiftly in your hand and begin to affect the temperature of the wine. You don't want to be warming up your chilled white now, do you?

Well, maybe you do, actually – if you think your wine is too cold. If so, by all means cup the bowl in your palm for a few minutes and warm it up a bit. That's totally acceptable.

It is a particular favourite pastime of wine pedants to point out incorrect holding of glassware. You see it on social media a bit. As with all knowledge, I think it's good to know what to do and why, but is rarely a good idea to use it to shame others. Hold your glass how you want, don't worry about what others are doing.

As well as keeping the wine at a steadier temperature, I like holding the stem as it lets you swirl the wine about with ease. You can sashay around the party much more louchely holding the stem than when wrapping your fist around the bowl.

How to Fill a Wine Glass

Ideally you should never fill a wine glass more than one-third full. You want a decent amount of space to allow you to swirl it about. The aromas released need space in the bowl to gather and you need space in your glass for your nose as you tilt it.

Pouring smaller quantities helps regulate the temperature in the glass, too – the wine doesn't hang about long enough to warm up too much. It also looks classier. Which is a terrible reason to do anything, but we're only human.

Opening a Bottle

You need a nice bottle opener. Nice doesn't mean expensive, but it does mean a Waiter's Friend. It can be a £5, super-basic model for all I care; it doesn't have to be *Forge de Laguiole*, but it should be a small, folding corkscrew with a tiny 'wine shank' knife at the end. That's my jam. I suggest it is your jam also. Rarely am I dogmatic about anything in wine, but when I have to use one of those horrible clunky bastards with two arms that raise up, it really winds me up. Maybe it's because I grew up in hospitality, I don't know.

Use the little serrated knife on the Waiter's Friend to cut the metal capsule, either above or below the small lip at the top. Now, check out the cork. Is it dry and old? Discoloured? Or does it look firm and plump and happy? A little discolouration is fine – especially with older bottles. Old corks can look mega funky, all black and mottled. Don't let it put you off. Proceed. Dry corks require a bit of TLC, though, to ease the corkscrew in without breaking them – just go very steady and try not to push down too much.

You want to screw the corkscrew into the centre of the cork gently, until you've gone the whole way in. Then gently prise the cork out. Don't bend the cork as you pull, or it may split in half. Use a nice gentle pulling motion.

With young wine, sling it about in any old position while doing this. If the wine is old, though, particularly with reds, it will likely have some sediment in the bottle, so keep it upright and as still as possible. See 'Decanting' (page 87) for next steps if sediment is present.

Once open, pour a little and give it a sniff – if it's nice, crack on. If not, give it five minutes in the glass. If it still smells a bit closed and funky, now is the time to assess whether it is good enough or faulty (see 'Wine Faults', page 97).

Opening Sparkling Wine

'Twist the bottle, not the cork.' The classic advice. I've never really understood this. I do a bit of both.

Sparkling needs to be well-chilled before opening. The carbon dioxide in the bubbles gets pretty volatile at room temperature, so opening un-chilled bottles with any kind of grace is next to impossible. Chill 'em.

The foil cap on the bottle neck will have a little pull-tab to help remove the top neatly, giving you access to the caged cork below. Unwind the cage until it's fully released, give it a little wiggle so it's free of the bottle. Keep your thumb over the cork the whole time so it can't suddenly pop out. You can remove the cage now, if you want, but I leave it on loosely for ease. Hold the cork firmly in one fist, the bottle firmly with the other hand at the base. The bottle should be at a thirty-degree angle, the more horizontal the better. Twist the base of the bottle and

the cork a little and you will feel it begin to give. If it isn't well chilled, you'll know about it now, as the cork will already have pushed its way out. Ease the cork out gently. The thirty-degree angle helps the cork come out gradually, an edge at a time, rather than vertically where it leaves the bottle all
at once.

Do it right and it will make a 'pssssst' sound. You are James Bond. Mostly it will make a distinct pop. Party's started. Win-win.

Opening Wax-sealed Wine

Wax seals are beautiful. A pain to apply, as the bottles are hand dipped in melted wax one at a time, but they function like a classic metal capsule, giving the cork protection, but not being airtight.

Don't start chopping at the wax with a knife, you'll just cut yourself and make a mess. Forget there's wax on there. Push a corkscrew through the middle of the wax into the cork. Continue to screw it gently into the cork and ease the cork out. The wax will give way as the cork is removed. You may need to pull a little half-broken wax from the lip of the bottle at the end to avoid drips.

Corks

Cork has been used to stopper wine for centuries. It has the enormous benefit of being porous enough to allow oxygen to gently interact with the wine, but not porous enough that wine seeps out. Cork's physical properties allow it to be inserted into the neck of the bottle and hold firmly without degrading over long periods of time.

Traditional corks come from the bark of the cork oak tree, grown mainly in Portugal and Spain. These trees have their bark removed once a decade. A process which causes them no issue and is positively regenerative, albeit relatively slow to establish. Top-quality traditional corks are punched out of whole segments of the bark. One single piece.

Most wines use agglomerated cork; the same cork bark but blitzed to tiny pieces and checked for traces of bacterial taint (see 'Wine Faults', page 97). These pieces are bonded back together into a cork shape using a food-grade glue. Each end of the cork has a thin disk of whole-punched cork attached, so it looks very similar to a traditional cork. They are cheaper, but can function equally well. There are cutting-edge 'technical corks' made like this today, offering winemakers options on oxygen ingress rates and all sorts.

In lower-priced wines you may find plastic replica corks. These are not designed for keeping the wine in the bottle for long, have less successful control over oxygen getting into the wine than 'proper' cork and are usually pretty horrible to pull out of the bottle to boot.

Corks are often more expensive for a winemaker than screw caps, although not always. They also carry the possibility of tainting the wine with trichloranisole (again, see 'Wine Faults', page 97), but the risk is very low.

I've Broken the Cork, What Do I Do?!

Swear liberally. Then try to twist your corkscrew into the remaining cork in the bottle neck. Sometimes you're lucky, with very minimal pushing and a good corkscrew you can usually get enough purchase to pull it out. Sorted.

If you can't, you have no option but to push the cork into the bottle with something long and thin. Next, you need to pour the wine into a clean jug, preferably through a thin muslin filter (coffee filters work a charm) to catch the bits of broken cork. If you can't do this, use the best sieve you have and fish out any remaining bits with clean fingers.

You can serve the wine from the jug, or rinse the bottle to remove any bits of cork, ensure it's empty of water and return the wine to the bottle.

Messy business.

Screw Caps: The Low Down

Screw caps have been used to seal wine since the late 1970s. While originally designed by a French company, they became synonymous in the early 2000s with New World wines. The perception was that screw caps were being used for lower-quality, fruit-driven wines, not wines with serious pedigree and complexity. However, Austria, Germany, New Zealand and Australia really got behind them at all quality levels and price points, pushing the conversation forward. There has been heated debate ever since between intensely boring people who really actually care how bottles of wine are closed.

Screw caps are now highly revered and are used by wineries the world over. There is no difference in potential quality between wines of either closure, although certain countries and wine styles do have their 'traditional' choice; be that New Zealand's screw caps or France's cork.

Screw caps have evolved in the forty plus years since they have been used for wine. They can now be purchased with specific levels of oxygen ingress, to allow bottle ageing.

Glass Stoppers

Oh, fuck them. Fiddly, style-over-substance pains in the arse. Watch out for your nails.

Sediment

Almost exclusively a red wine phenomenon. Sediment is the silty, tiny particles that sometimes form in a wine as it ages. They build up along the edge of a bottle, as it lies on its side. It is microscopic debris of grape skins and yeasts that have bound together, alongside some tannin and colour molecules that also bind to form larger particles. Sediment is harmless but, ultimately, not something most drinkers want in their mouth while enjoying a glass of wine.

Decanting

The act of transferring the wine from its old bottle to a new container – usually to remove sediment. It takes a little preparation. It's all about the theatre.

Gently, stand the wine up on its base for a day (or a few, ideally) so the sediment slowly falls to the bottom of the bottle. If you don't have the luxury of a few days, just stand it up for as long as possible.

Open the bottle gently, leaving it standing vertically.

Prepare a jug or a nice glass decanter if you have one. Ensure it's clean and free of residual washing up liquid and dust. You can put a filter in the neck of the decanter, but I think that's cheating. Set a candle (or use the torch on your phone) next to the decanter, so there is a good, clear source of light.

Pick up the bottle gently in one hand, and the jug in the other. Hold both over the source of light, tilting the jug so the wine will pour down the sides in a thin stream. Very slowly pour the wine in one motion into the jug. Watch carefully as you pour a slow, steady trickle of wine into the jug. As it falls down the sides, you will see the wine pouring clearly. Continue pouring until you see little bits of sediment begin to enter the jug's stream. Immediately stop pouring. This should be quite close to the end of the bottle, if done correctly.

You can use a filter for the final little bit of wine, if you have one. Or, leave it. I usually pour it carefully into a separate glass to try and have a little sneak peak of the wine without too much sediment being in there!

Note: You can decant any wine, whether it has sediment or not. Almost all wine opens up a little and becomes more expressive more swiftly when in a decanter. In these cases, don't pour slowly, just crack the bottle and pour it liberally into the decanter or jug. Sorted.

Keeping Wine Once Opened

Open wine lasts longer than many people expect. The general rule is, open the bottle as few times as possible. The more wine in the bottle, the better protected it will be. Keep it in the fridge, as this slows the degradation. This goes for reds, too. Fridge them, then bring them out to return to a nice serving temperature before drinking.

Wines that can last longest once opened are fresh, clean, higher-acid whites; leaner styles of oak-aged whites; and reds with good acidity and concentrated fruit. Higher levels of acidity, alcohol and tannin really help to protect a wine once opened.

There are some wines that are nearly indestructible and can be left open at room temperature indefinitely; the oxidised and 'maderised' (uniquely warmed during ageing) fortified wines of Madeira and those of Marsala are the two best-known examples.

Floral, aromatic whites and perfumed reds, especially with lower alcohol or lower acidity are the quickest to lose their edge, becoming a bit flabby and inexpressive after a few days in the fridge.

Sparkling wine and Champagne are surprisingly great at staying in good shape once opened. They are typically in the fresh, clean, high-acid white category and the carbon dioxide helps. Even more so than with still wines, the more wine left in the bottle the better. If you only have a glass or so left in the bottle, just drink it. It isn't going to survive the night with much fizz remaining. There are fantastic sparkling wine stoppers on the market; usually for only about £5. Every sparkling wine brand has branded ones for sale at their winery, too. Most work brilliantly and are really useful. Definitely invest.

I'm sorry to say it but the teaspoon in the bottle trick doesn't work. There it is. I thought I'd rip the plaster off quickly, rather than making a scene. I have no idea where this came from, but I've seen no evidence to support it. If you don't have a stopper, by all means pop a spoon in there if it makes you feel good, but you might as well leave it open. A half-full bottle of sparkling left without a stopper should be okay the next day, if a little less fizzy. You can cling film the top and secure it with a rubber band, if you want to get all Art Attack about it.

SERVING TEMPERATURE – THE NUMBERS				
Sparkling and Dessert Wine	Light White and Rosé Wine	Full-bodied White, Oak-aged or Mature Wine	Light Red Wine	Fuller Red, Oak-aged or Mature Wine
6–10°C	7–11°C	9–12°C	11–16°C	16–19°C

Specific wine temperature is one of the most common 'facts' that I am asked for. I oblige willingly but always wonder what the people are doing when they get home. Dipping a thermometer in every glass of wine? Fair enough, if so, but that sounds stressful. Antithetical to the simple joy of the act. I think we preoccupy ourselves with this part of wine, especially if we don't feel confident. Nailing the serving temperature feels a rare opportunity for us to have some control over the otherwise aloof bottle. It's comforting to know we've done our bit right. A sense of responsibility to the wine, to the guest, to ourselves as good hosts. Be aware of it, but try to let that sense of responsibility dissipate, I'd say.

The temperatures given are correct but different wines reach their absolute peak for enjoyment at different temperatures. But I don't think about it in numbers. Ever. Whites and rosés cooler, reds a bit warmer. The leaner and fresher styles of any colour tend to benefit from being cooler. The fuller, richer styles, the opposite. Most wine temperature issues can be allayed with the phrase, and remember this: 'Sorry, it's only been in the fridge for twenty but let's have a quick splash and chuck it back in, shall we?' I have never had a response other than 'Yes!' with a wry smile. What rogues we are! It's fun, it's shared culpability for a little naughtiness, it's sociable. Everything wine should be.

If you drink wine regularly with a little consciousness, you'll swiftly pick up a good natural gauge of the 'right' temperature. You'll become a wine temperature diviner, reading wines like braille through your nose and mouth, aware the temperature is a bit off-the-ideal before you've even put glass to lips.

The thing with temperature and wine is this – colder temperatures make wines feel leaner, fresher, crisper. They reduce a wine's alcoholic warmth. You simply get less aroma and flavour the colder you go. Warmer temperatures promote richer, fuller character. The ripe fruit will appear bolder, alcohol the more obvious, nothing is hidden, everything is open and lifting from the glass readily.

A light white wine plucked from the supermarket shelf will taste much weightier, more alcoholic, more ripe if you crack it open immediately. Security will also ask you to leave, in my experience. There is a general truth that we commonly serve white wines too cold and red wines too warm. This fertile ground for wine pedantry can be navigated easily with the following approach:

- If you're social drinking, all the best, easy-drinking white, rosé and sparkling wines can be served directly from the fridge. Fridge them for a few hours or ice bucket them and serve from there. The wine may be a touch too chilly on serving, but will quickly warm in the glass. People want refreshment.

- If you're sitting to eat or consciously tasting a wine, fully chill white, rosé and sparkling. Bring them out twenty minutes or a little more before serving and leave them on the table. They'll be nicely cool but more open and characterful to taste.

- Modern room temperature is usually a bit too warm for reds. It isn't essential, but if you can, bang fuller, richer styles (like Bordeaux, Malbec, Cabernet Sauvignon) in the fridge or an ice bucket for ten minutes or so before serving, just to nudge the temperature down a bit. A very slightly cool sensation is pleasant with all reds as they hit your palate. For really light, fresh reds (Beaujolais, modern Grenache, etc.), treat them like dark rosé and chill them well, then give them twenty minutes out of the fridge before drinking.

As a final note, it is always preferable for a wine to be too cold than too warm. You can quickly warm a too-cool wine by cupping the bowl of the glass in your hands. A few minutes will really make a difference. A too-warm wine is a lecherous, peacock of a thing. Keep it at arm's length.

Ice Buckets – How to Use One Effectively

Fridges are the standard, right? We have a gauge for how quickly they chill things. We use them every day. It takes an hour or two to chill a bottle effectively. Freezers can be quick alternatives, but you run the risk of forgetting the bottle and ruining it.

If you really want to get a wine cold quickly or chill lots of bottles at once, you need ice. But, crucially, ice alone isn't going to do the trick. A bottle packed in with ice cubes chills quite slowly due to the relatively small surface area of the bottle in contact with the cubes. You need water. Half fill your bucket, sink, deep saucepan, whatever, with ice cubes. Then slosh in a decent amount of water – enough so that when you put bottles in, they are well submerged. Now the entire surface area of the bottle is in contact with icy water. Fifteen minutes of that will have your white approaching serving temperature, thirty will have it nailed.

Need to move faster? A restaurant trick is to throw salt into the ice bucket, reducing the freezing temperature of the water and allowing it to get even colder. The ice will melt faster but the water will get colder. Keep topping the ice up, if you have enough.

Even faster? Spin the bottle regularly. This moves the wine inside the bottle, bringing more wine in contact with the cold glass. You can get a room temperature bottle down to a reasonable serving temperature in sub-ten minutes, if you deploy the salt and spin trick.

Ice in Your Wine Glass

It's fine. You do you. I don't do it, unless it's rosé and outra-geously sunny and I have a thirst on. The concern with putting ice in wine is partly temperature but more about dilution. The best thing to do is either use a very large ice cube, like the ones used in short cocktails, or fill your glass with lots of ice cubes. Both chill the wine swiftly, while minimising the amount the ice melts. Then, drink fast.

Storing Wine

In the dream scenario, wine is stored lying on its side, at a constant temperature between 11–14°C, in fifty to seventy per cent humidity and complete darkness. This is achievable in professional storage units or specialist wine storage at home. If you are spending lots of money on wine to lay down for many years, it's worth investing in a specialist storage unit.

For most people, the best solution is finding the coolest spot in your house that has the least variance in temperature – under the stairs and under your bed are two great spots. It will be warmer than 11–14°C but, as long as it's below about 22°C most of the time, the wine shouldn't oxidise and degrade at any major rate. You can safely store wines in this state for many years without much issue. Slightly warmer temperatures for long periods (a year or more) can cause wines to taste dull and 'cooked' – dried fruits and baked characters. They lose their finesse.

Garages and uninsulated outbuildings are not great for storing wine for long periods, even though they are usually cooler than indoors, as the temperature fluctuates dramatically between day and night. With the season changes, it can also get well above that 22°C maximum. Better to store it somewhere with fewer changes in temperature, even if the base temperature is slightly warmer. Variable temperature can push corks out or cause leaks, as the wine inside contracts and grows in volume as temperatures flex.

The number one thing to be aware of, and something that is much more controllable than the absolute temperature, is UV light. You don't want it. The main offender here is sunlight, but fluorescent bulbs give off some, too. Store wines in their boxes or a space without light. 'Light strike' caused by UV happens quickly (within hours!) in bright light or very slowly if small amounts of UV are present over time. It causes dulling of the wine's flavour and the development of horrible, eggy, oniony, cabbagey characters. Grim. So don't store wines in those nice open wine racks under the window, please.

Don't worry about the humidity level when you're storing wine at home over a few years; it's unlikely your home will be far outside the fifty to seventy per cent ideal range. Very rarely does this come up as a hazard.

Storing bottles on their side – horizontally – is key, though. This keeps the wine in contact with the cork, which keeps the cork moist and the closure in good condition. Corks dry out quickly, if the bottle stands vertically. Once dry, corks let oxygen in fast. Only stand bottles vertically if you plan to drink them within a few weeks. Screw caps and other closures don't need to be horizontal, so store them in any orientation you like.

Regular vibrations are potentially bad for wine over long durations. It is thought that shaking up the molecules speeds the chemical reactions taking place and hastens the ageing process. Like humidity, this is rarely an issue when storing at home, but perhaps don't store your bottles somewhere they'll get constantly moved or jumped around on.

If you are building up a bit of a wine collection, you'll soon meet modern bits of equipment, like Coravin, which allow you to pour glasses of cork-stoppered bottles without opening the bottle. They use a needle to extract the wine and pump inert gas, such as argon, into the void to keep the wine protected. I use one and really like it. It's expensive – not just the unit itself, but the gas refills are about £0.50 per 125ml glass, I reckon – but it is effective and allows me to have a single glass of something *really* nice, which is often all I want. That said, I am not sure if I would be brave enough to use one on a rare, sentimental bottle intended for long, further ageing. I use it on wines I want to drink over months or within a year.

Glass Bottles and Other Vessels: How We Got Here and Where We're Going

For a bunch of centuries, back in the day, we would have rocked up to the party with our earthenware jugs. One or two legends would sneak in an animal-skin pouch filled to bursting for the afters. Snazzy. We filled those smaller vessels from an enormous clay pot buried in the ground of our house (if we were lucky!). We used that pot for longer-term storage. Oh, the heady days of circa 6000–2500 BC.

Glass first made an appearance around 3000 BC. Many civilisations used glass but it was hugely fragile and totally unsuitable for transporting wine, so earthenware pots continued to be the vogue. At the occasional properly bougie Greek and Roman gathering, though, circa 1500 BC and onwards, you'd find people decanting wines into ornamental glass bottles to serve or store wine for short periods. Glass and wine were beginning their courtship.

In 250 AD, give or take a hundred years, Gaul (now France) was really coming up on the wine scene. Influenced largely by the Gauls and Romans, many of us gradually started storing our wines in wooden barrels. Less fragile, for sure, but hardly easier to transport. They had the unfortunate habit of oxidising and turning the wine to vinegar, too. In fact, much more so than the clay amphora, unless they were studiously sealed and kept topped up. Yeah, I'll admit it, it wasn't always in the best condition. But, hey, neither were we! We made the best of it. The party continued.

It was the seventeenth century when coal fire gave us the potential to make glass tough enough for longer-term storage and the safe transport of wine. From this point on, slowly but surely, wine began to be bottled in glass. Initially, bottling was done by the wine shippers, who would import the casks of wine, typically sell the whole cask to their customer and then bottle said cask for their consumption. Bottles were not a standard size at this point – that came much later. It wasn't until the mid-1800s that individual glass bottles of wine were readily available for sale. And it is only in the last century that wineries themselves have increasingly bottled their own wine, on-site at the winery, to control quality and assure provenance.

Glass bottles are brilliant for storing and ageing wine. They are pretty sturdy and are a nice shareable size, which is so much a part of wine's charm. Sure, they let UV light in, but we have developed dark glass, which helps a bit. Their design has evolved to be longer and thinner, for easier storage and most are strengthened by the punt – that concave dimple at the base of most bottles. They're fab. That is, until you consider their weight. Glass is heavy. Today the glass bottle's weight is a major problem. Their easy recyclability is a plus, but the use of excess resources to produce an organoleptically pleasing but totally frivolous single-use heavy bottle feels like something from a bygone era. More so, transporting cases of glass bottles around the world is far from efficient. In fact, it's a sustainability nightmare. Most 'everyday quality' wine is transported globally in bulk tanks now, and bottled in the country in which it is sold. This helps, but there are lighter, much more space-efficient ways of packaging wine available.

Don't get me wrong, I think the theatre and tradition of the glass bottle is something we should retain. I also think that any wine that improves in the bottle and has potential to age for many years is a totally valid use of glass. But we should consider changing the format for the easy-drinking, younger styles of wine we tend to have as our 'everyday'. If most wine we buy is only a year or two old and eighty-five per cent is drunk within forty-eight hours of purchase, heavy glass bottles for every 750ml of that begins to feel a bit gauche.

So, what are the options? Cans. Aluminium cans. Fully recyclable, albeit aluminium isn't an endless resource. With the advances in recent years in the lining inside the cans, allowing longer term storage of wine, they are a fantastic format. Single-serve sizing allows minimal waste, they are lightweight, stackable for transportation and, crucially, preserve the nuanced, detailed aromatics of wine well. I am a big fan. I have put them on restaurant wine lists (yes, really!), use them in my home and get excited about their potential.

There is also bag-in-box. Increasingly, these are made with plastic bags that are recyclable (albeit at specialist recycling places) and have easily recyclable cardboard outers. Lightweight and efficient to transport, they fit in the fridge nicely and are convenient for festivals and outdoor drinks. Most now boast six weeks' or so lifespan from opening. That's pretty good. We will see lots more, premium-quality bag-in-box in the coming years, I am certain.

Don't be afraid of alternative formats. Let's go out there together and explore. The days of cans and bag-in-box being synonymous with crap wine are behind us. Wine on tap, a big thing now in many cities across the world, is no bad thing either. Served from kegs, like beer, they can be decent quality and it's a perfect delivery system for good plonk on a night out.

Wine Faults

I often say there is no right or wrong in wine. That tasting is subjective and we each appreciate something different. This is absolutely true, until you encounter 'a fault'. We're not talking about slightly too high acidity, or overly bitter tannin here – those are subjective, to a degree, and depend on what you're eating, your personal preference, etc. Faults are objectively horrible characters that are not supposed to be present.

Faults are usually caused by a bacterial infection, the presence of certain undesirable yeasts, or too much or too little contact with oxygen. They are highly unlikely to make you ill – wine's natural mix of alcohol and acidity really helps mitigate that risk.

In a restaurant, you can send a bottle back if you think it's faulty. By all means, ask the waiter's opinion, if you like, but if the wine doesn't smell right to you, you can politely request to have another. You can return faulty bottles to wine shops and supermarkets, too, providing you haven't finished the bottle. Return it with wine still present so the retailer can assess it. Unless the wine was particularly mature and 'sold as seen' (i.e. you knew there was a risk of oxidation), then most will be glad to refund or replace.

Poor old corks get a lot of the blame for faulty wines. It's true that an increasingly rare but common-enough wine fault is 'mustiness' or 'cork taint', which you will encounter on occasion if you drink wine regularly. A compound called trichloranisole (TCA) can exist in poor-quality cork. While corks are the usual culprit, TCA can also come from incorrectly cleaned wood barrels in the winery, so it's not always the cork's fault. TCA gives wine a very noticeable musty, mushroomy, wet cardboard sort of character. You'll notice it on the nose if it's present and it will likely be so off-putting you won't need to taste it! TCA isn't harmful; it's just foul. It's also very disruptive in the short-term to your sense of smell and taste, so make sure to get the bottle away and wash your glass thoroughly before pouring the next one.

Oxidation is a natural part of maturing wine. It becomes a fault if it overpowers the wine's character. White wines go yellow or brown and lose their vibrancy and fruit. Red wines become paler and gain an orangey, brown rim. All wines get a toffee, nutty, dull character if oxidation is too present.

Reduction is a fault that is the polar opposite of oxidation. This is where a wine has received too little oxygen in the winemaking process, which causes eggy, sulphurous aromas to form in the wine. The wine's bright, fruity character is dulled and the dirty-drains character sits on top of it all. Not good when it overtakes the wine, but in tiny doses it can add gunflint, struck-match subtle notes, which can be quite enticing in some wines, like Burgundian Chardonnay or English Bacchus.

Myriad other possible wine faults exist, but those are some of the most common ones.

5.

Food and Wine

To have a love of wine without a love of food is rare. Many people come to wine through their interest in food. They are complementary passions, peas in a pod. The act of bringing them together is natural and instinctive. It can also be daunting. This is definitely an area of wine that many assume can be done 'wrong'. It can certainly be overcomplicated. There are definitely some traditional 'rules' that we feel under pressure to follow.

Wine and food matching is polarising. Some think of it as they may do homeopathy or biodynamics, a pseudo-science with little empirical evidence for its claimed virtues. Others are fully convinced in its principles and make it the centre point of their wine enjoyment, carefully picking specific wines to serve with specific dishes, seeking gastronomic nirvana. As ever, I think the best place to be is somewhere in the middle.

There is no doubt that there are combinations of wine and food that elevate the sensory experience of both. Anyone who has had fish and chips with English sparkling wine, or a beefy Malbec with ribeye can sense this, surely? This is the nirvana those advocates are looking for – the meeting point where the food brings out a hidden quality in the wine and the wine balances a note in the dish so it is at its absolute peak. Two things coming together, one chewier than the other, combining to be greater than the sum of their parts.

Growing up in pubs and restaurants, I spent my formative years building a natural awareness of successful combinations of food and drink. It becomes second nature. Like cooking without a recipe. The more you do it, the more confident you become at judging the level of seasoning and searing and stirring required. You begin to have a keen awareness of what complements what. You gauge quickly what might be an absolute clanger. I think this approach, one of natural exploration, is the right one for wine and food. Not overcomplicating it, being open to a little trial and error. I have picked up some tips and tricks along the way that will help you in this life-long journey of discovery.

The Three Types of Food and Wine Pairing

There are three basic types of food and wine pairing – complementary, contrasting and geographical. Most successful matches fall neatly into one of these. I find it helps to consider which of these you are hoping to achieve before setting off.

Complementary Pairings

Where the wine and food share a key characteristic. Each bringing something similar to the table. When put together, they bump up alongside each other and there is natural harmony.

Take, for example, ceviche and Albariño. Both food and wine hang on a citrus acidity, they fall in line together and hold one another up. Sticky toffee pudding and Pedro Ximenez sherry is another. They both bring unctuous sweetness, and the toffee falls in line with PX's ultra-sweet raisin fruit.

As lovely as these pairings are, they can be really tricky to pull off successfully. They hinge on getting the intensity of each component in balance. When it works, though, it's electric.

Contrasting Pairings

The opposite of complementary pairings. Here, the wine and food contrast one another. Each brings characteristics lacking in its partner. Together they find balance.

Great examples would be crispy roast pork belly with a freshly acidic German Riesling, or salty, tangy blue cheese with a honeyed, sweet Sauternes. The food and wine don't share a dominant flavour, rather each has quite a pronounced character of its own. By bringing together two opposing tastes, they meet in the middle and find harmony.

Geographical Pairings

A bit hit and miss this one, I won't lie. More often than not the thinking is 'What grows together, goes together.'
The core wine concept of terroir applies to other things, too. You find terroir with cheese, for example. The animal eats the grass of its region, which has distinct characteristics and a seasonality to it, this in turn affects the milk's flavour and, thus, the resulting cheese carries both a sense of place and of time of year. This sense of location can sometimes allow harmonious matches between different local products.

In addition to a shared terroir, there is a social phenomenon that occurs in regions the world over. Farmers and winemakers growing up together, sharing dining tables as friends and families, over many generations, often begin to craft produce that combine well together. It makes sense that if I am eating my neighbour's fresh, lemony-herby goat's cheese on the regular, I might, consciously or not, start making my wine in such a way that it is complementary. The wines and cheeses of the Loire Valley are an example of exactly this. For this reason, if all else fails and you get stuck, try the local foods with the local wines and, more often than not, it results in something brilliant.

The Rules of Pairing

Once you've considered which type of pairing you're going with, the success of the pairing relies on balancing the key characteristics of both wine and food. This is where lots of the traditional 'rules' around wine and food pairing come in to play. As you'll see, though, there is nuance and opportunity for experimentation here. Nothing is set in stone.

Flavour Intensity

How flavourful and intense is the dish or wine? An intensely flavoured, powerful dish requires a wine with a similar level of intensity, otherwise it will get lost. A light, delicate dish requires a wine of equal elegance and finesse, or the wine will overwhelm.

A grilled Dover sole with butter and lemon is a beautiful thing. One of the most delicately flavoured, fantastically simple dishes imaginable. A bombastic, ripe, aromatically intense white wine would mask it completely. So, a lower flavour intensity Chablis or something similar might work a charm.

Structural Intensity

Flavour intensity is obvious but equally important is structural intensity. How does the wine 'feel' in the mouth? What sensation does it evoke?

A Californian Chardonnay, matured in oak, might be only moderately intensely flavoured, but it is probably a rich, buttery, full-bodied and gently oak-tannin bitter thing structurally. Taking our Dover sole example, it might well overwhelm the subtle, flaky texture of the fish. Equally, higher-acid wines, such as Albarino, have a sensation of leaner, finer structure. Ideal with the Dover sole as it replicates the lemon juice classic accompaniment. Refreshing the palate, not dominating.

Red wines tend to have greater sensation of structural intensity than whites. The skin contact in their production brings tannin to a greater or lesser degree. This is why there is a general idea that we have whites before reds (lighter first, moving to richer) and why whites tend to be the traditional pairing with lighter-styled dishes. There is truth here, but it is much more nuanced than the 'only white wine with fish' brigade would like to admit. Low-tannin, fresher-acidity red wines (Beaujolais, some Mencía, Pinot Noir, for example) might be ideal with some fish dishes, if their structural intensity matches.

Sweetness

A little sweetness is a really helpful thing for food and wine pairing, even if it's just the sunny, ripe character in a dry wine from a warm climate. Dishes with a little sweetness – tomatoes, say – find wines with a little sweet note easy to sit alongside. Salty foods love sweetness in wine, too, as it creates a nice push-pull contrasting character; think salty and sweet popcorn.

Ideally, every pairing will have a wine that is very (very!) slightly sweeter than the dish it is with. If the dish is sweeter than the wine, it makes the wine taste thinner and more astringent. The good news is, most wines naturally have a little sugar kicking about.

At the very sweet end of the food spectrum, the rule of having wine sweeter than the dish is even more important. Think Tokaji, Pedro Ximénez, Rutherglen Muscat.

Aciiiiiiid!

A key component in all wine, acidity is an important consideration when picking your pairing. Acidity in a wine is your friend both in complementary and contrasting pairings. Alongside a dish with acidity (lamb with a vinegary mint sauce or a lemon tart, for example), finding a wine with equal acidity will give it complementary harmony. Equally, acidity in wine LOVES fat and salt (much like all of my favourite people). Acidity cuts through fats and refreshes the palate. Alongside salt, it creates an electric buzz. Think salt and vinegar crisps. Acidic wines, like Champagne, Assyrtiko and Barbera, are great, therefore, with deep-fried dishes. Fizz and fried chicken is every sommelier's go-to, after-work pick-me-up.

Tannin

It's worth bearing tannins in mind when considering pairings. Whether it's a subtly skin-contact-influenced white, a more grippy orange wine, or a deep, brooding red, any tannin present has an impact on the wine's appropriateness to pair with food.

Most importantly, tannins bind with protein molecules. This means that tannic wines are enormously beneficial in pairing with higher protein dishes. The classic pairing of a Cabernet-Sauvignon-rich Claret with roast beef became a classic precisely because the tannins in the wine structurally match well with the dense meat and, in turn, the protein-rich meat reduces the sensation of bitter tannin in the wine.

So, the more tannic the wine, the more protein-rich the dish should be (whether animal or plant based).

Interestingly, the combination of tannin and fish oil is a rare case of food and wine pairings producing an actually unpleasant sensation. Heavy tannin and oily fish combine to create a metallic taste, a little like licking a battery. This is why it is rare to find heavy red wines served alongside fish dishes and is the basis of the tradition of only serving white or pale rosé with fish. As discussed, a little tannin with fish is usually fine, so light reds and deep rosés, particularly from the fridge, can be perfect partners, too.

Wine and Cheese

No introduction to wine and food pairing would be complete without a note about wine and cheese. Of all the pairings, perhaps this is the most iconic.

The classic image of wine and cheese together, depicted everywhere from grandparents' dining-table place mats to artisan food magazine front covers, tends to be a bottle of red wine and a cheeseboard laden with blue, Cheddar and something creamy. I'm afraid that image is a lie.

Red wine is an absolute bastard to pair with most cheeses. The bitter tannin plays havoc with the delicate creamy textures of the cheese. The cheese's lactic, mouth-coating creaminess makes even the best red taste a bit simple. I concede a nice mature Cheddar and a bold red wine can be incredible, but that's just it; it must be a bold, hopefully relatively sweet, intensely flavoured red wine to get away with it. That's why Port works so well!

Much better to have a white. Nice, fresh, clean-acid white. The acidity refreshes the palate from all that lactic behaviour, intense citrus and concentrated orchard fruit characters rub up alongside the often gently citrussy, herby notes in the cheese itself. Refreshing.

Sweetness in the wine is hugely beneficial, too, whether white or red. Sweetness brings the wine's structural weight up to the cheese's and pushes back against the natural acidity found in many of them.

A key thing to bear in mind is that cheese and wine age in the opposite way to one another. As a wine ages, its tannins soften, its acidity gently declines, its fruit flavours mature and dry a little and lose their 'crunch'. The older a wine, the more delicate and nuanced and gentle it becomes. Cheese starts life as creamy, soft and subtle as it will ever be. As it ages, it loses water through evaporation, concentrating the acidity, salts and flavour. A mature cheese is crunchier, more acidic and more intense than ever. So, old wine stands a better chance with younger, milder cheese. Mature cheeses demand bright, flavourful, juicy young wines.

You could spend hours joyfully pairing specific wines with specific cheeses but, really, who has the time? My go-to if I'm putting wine out with a big, mixed cheeseboard – at Christmas, it's just Christmas, basically – is to pick one or two of the following, each of which are the best all-rounder wines:

- Champagne or another Traditional Method sparkling wine – acidity and bubbles refresh you, flavours should be in that citrus and orchard spectrum, crucially they often have quite a bit of sugar hiding in there.

- Port & Sherry – either intense, bold Vintage Port or nutty, complex Tawny Port styles. Or, rich, flavourful, off-dry / medium-sweet sherry styles like Palo Cortado or Amontillado.

- A sweet, but not lusciously sweet, botrytis-spiced dessert wine, like Sauternes or Monbazillac – either of those will nail almost any cheese situation. Done.

6.

How to Read a Wine Label

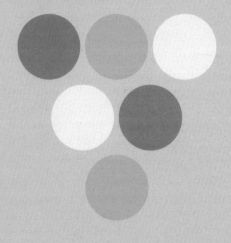

Wine bottle labels are not necessarily the easiest things to navigate. Part of the charm of choosing a bottle is the sense of adventure. Will it be delicious? What will it taste like? It is both reassuring and helpful to feel, at least to a certain degree, that you can speak the language of wine, digest the general vibe and decipher the lingo dotted about on a label.

So, let's look at the key things you find on a wine bottle label. Even without a detailed description from the winery's marketing department on the reverse, you can do your best Inspector Clouseau impression and make some observations.

The Vibe

Every wine bottle has been intentionally designed. Even the most traditional label, essentially unchanged for a hundred years, has had someone give it very close attention and a nip and a tuck here and there. If these people have done their job even remotely well, you will gain an immediate sense of the style and character of the wine just by glancing at it. Bright, fun, modern designs speak of similarly positioned wines inside. Traditional line-drawn pictures of a chateau on an off-white label speak to sophistication and complexity. Straight-shooting minimalism, the same in the liquid.

Don't overthink it, though, just let yourself pick up the cues. Gut instinct should lead you to select a particular bottle. Once it's in your grip, there are some key bits of information you can easily glean that will further help you vet your choice.

Country of Origin

The label will always tell you the country of origin, usually with a bit more detail, sometimes down to specific vineyards.

Time to generalise! As you know, lighter, fresher wines typically come from cooler regions. Consider the general climate of the country or area the wine comes from; the warmer it is, the more likely the wine will be fuller bodied with riper, bolder fruit flavours.

The more wine you taste and the greater the amount of knowledge you accrue about specific wine regions, the more informed this becomes, but thinking from a broad country-wide basis is a good place to start.

Appellations – Defined Wine Regions

Wine region names are protected in law. The legislation protects the tradition and identity of food and drink products of geographical origin. It also serves to protect consumers, ensuring the product is authentic and is actually from where it says it is. If a producer wants to name a specific wine region on the label – in fact, if they want to give any more geographical detail than just the country of origin, 'Vin de France' for example – then they need to conform to the agreed rules governing the specific geographical designation. These defined wine areas are often referred to as appellations.

Every country has its own system but they all run broadly in the same way. The region's boundaries are drawn up, and within each region there should be a clear, unique geographic and climatic character that sets it apart from its neighbours. A set of rules governing the permitted vineyard and winemaking practices and, often, the allowed grape varietals are defined, too. All grapes must be sourced from within the defined region (well, actually, there is usually fifteen per cent wiggle room . . .).

The wine region name becomes a brand. To be able to use the brand on their label, producers must conform to the rules. In some regions, the governing authority tastes and checks wines for their quality and 'typicity' prior to approving their use of the appellation.

There is often a hierarchy among regional brands. At the top, there are iconic, smaller regions, sometimes covering little more than a single vineyard, or perhaps a group of vineyards with a specific microclimate. These are areas with the longest wine heritage, the most highly regarded vineyards, producing wines with a definitive character or identity. These will often have the most stringent rules, aimed at safeguarding the traditional style of the area, such as Sancerre in France or Chianti Classico DOCG in Tuscany.

Then, there is a second and third tier. These are increasingly wide geographical areas, the boundaries of which often overlap and fully contain the higher tier smaller regions within them. These larger areas will have an identity and definitive style of their own, but less specifically than the tier above. They often have increasingly less stringent rules on winemaking and a wider range of permitted grape varieties the further down the hierarchy you go. This might be the Loire Valley or Chianti DOC, large areas which themselves incorporate the previously mentioned Sancerre and Chianti Classico DOCG areas within their boundaries.

It is possible, therefore, for a producer to make a wine in a vineyard classified as a highest-tier appellation, but with a grape variety that is not permitted. In this instance, if the lower-tier classifications permit the variety, then they could use that lower-tier regional brand on the label instead. This kind of boundary-pushing behaviour is what often drives classic wine regions forwards. Over time, the rules may adapt to allow new varietals and winemaking techniques, if they are proven successful. If neither regional classification permits the winemaker's chosen grape variety and/or winemaking technique, they can fall back on a simple country of origin label. Wines in this lowest definition category are often referred to as 'table wines', due to them being usually simple, easy-drinking, cheap wines.

Certification applies wine by wine, rather than it being the producer themselves who is classified, so you often find a producer making top-tier appellation wines, as well as lower-tier appellation wines within their portfolio.

You can expect to pay more for higher-tier wines. They are scarcer, being from a small area, and they offer the experience of tasting a specific terroir. They are in high demand due to their fame. But, they are not always 'better' than the lower-tier wines. Lower tiers may include some larger-volume, everyday quality wine for sure (which is often what we're after), but they also include the creative, boundary-pushing winemakers keen to make their mark, unrestrained by often archaic legislation. Wines made under the wider appellation rules by iconic producers can often represent great value and exciting drinking.

Many non-European wine regions have simplified systems. Here they do not necessarily order regions into a perceived quality hierarchy. They simply have defined appellations with distinct geographic and climatic character. They may not be prescriptive about the grape varietals allowed. They may or may not control the allowed vineyard and winemaking practices. They tend to embrace a wider diversity of style and celebrate winemakers' opportunity to experiment, but equally want to ensure that you, as a consumer, can navigate the geography with ease. America, New Zealand and Australia are prime examples of this sort of modern approach.

WINE REGION APPELLATIONS AND LABELLING – MORE DETAIL

Some common examples of appellation tiers, in ascending order from the most stringent and top-tier, to the more loose and wide-ranging regional brands.

EU AND UK

Wines of geographic origin:

Protected Designation of Origin (PDO)

Protected Geographic Indication (PGI)

Below these are wines without a geographic origin – just naming the country

These form the basic, standardised EU framework for regional labelling. Each EU country uses their own terminology and some segment the PDO category into further tiers of quality, too. Examples overleaf.

ITALY

Denominazione di Origine Controllata e Garantita (DOCG) – small, particularly iconic sites within classic regions. There are very few. The best of the best

Denominazione di Origine Controllata (DOC) – PDO quality, clearly defined regions

Indicazione Geografica Tipica (IGT) – wider geographic regions. Less stringent rules

Vino da Tavola (VdT) – wine of country origin only

FRANCE

Appellation d'Origine Contrôlée (AOC)/Appellation d'Origine Protégée (AOP) – AOC/AOP interchangeable on labels. Top-tier, tightly defined regions. Some are tiny (La Romanée is 0.8 hectares in size), some much larger (Bordeaux is 111,000 hectares at time of writing)

Indication Géographique Protégée (IGP) – wider defined geographic regions, less stringent rules, more scope to experiment

Vin de France

USA

American Viticultural Area (AVA) – a defined region with clear unique geographic and climatic qualities. Not prescriptive over techniques and grape varietals

Producer Name

Whether a producer or a brand name, everything from the font to the name itself could give an indication of the wine style. 'Juicy Boy Vinho' sounds awful, but it probably tells you something about the wine inside.

If you've heard of the producer and know their style, that's a hefty leg-up. If you don't, try to remember it; you'll quickly build your mind map of the wine world that way.

Opening-price-point wines from famous producers are often great value. Perhaps the wine in particular comes from a less famous or less rigorously defined appellation, but all the same quality of winemaking and experience will be on display as with the producers' top price wines.

Wine Name

In addition to the producer or brand name, many wines have a name to differentiate them within the wider brand's range. If so, does the name give away anything about the wine's character?

Mentions of fog, sea breezes, mountains and coastlines might indicate it's a cooler-climate wine. Mentions of sunshine and great plains tell you it's more likely in-land and warmer-climate. Old vines (*vielles vignes, vinhas velhas,* etc.) speaks to complexity and intensity of fruit.

Vintage (Year)

The year of production – when the grapes were picked. If a wine does not display this, it means it could be a blend of multiple years – rare in still wines, but common in sparkling wines. It isn't an indication of poor quality to be NV (non-vintage) in sparkling and certain, relatively rare, artisanal styles of still wine, but it may indicate a lower-quality, big-volume production wine in lower-priced still wines.

It is typical for a northern hemisphere winery's new vintage wines to appear around March and the southern hemisphere's earliest new vintage wines to arrive on shop shelves around August. How close you are to those times of year will indicate how fresh and zippy the wine may be; wine styles made to be drunk young and fresh will be best within a year or so of release, other styles benefit from time in the bottle.

Some people have an encyclopaedic memory for 'good' vintages and instant recall. The more you can retain, obviously the better, but Google is your friend here.

All things aside, some of the nicest wine moments for me have been tasting birth-year wines (I am lucky, 1990 was a banger in many key places). The vintage on a bottle gives you an opportunity to buy someone a heartful present, should you want to.

Alcohol Level

Displayed as % vol or ABV (alcohol by volume), it refers to the proportion of the total liquid that is pure alcohol. Depending on the country of sale, there is usually a small margin for error in the percentage stated on the bottle. For wine in the UK, EU and USA it is between 0.5 and 1.5 per cent, depending on wine strength, so it's not an exact art, but you can be sure it's a close, representative value. One per cent or so can sound small in terms of a wine's alcoholic potency, but it is actually quite significant – a couple of glasses of 11.5 per cent compared to 14.5 per cent wine can have quite different effects!

The more alcohol in a wine, the more robust and full-bodied it will taste. Less alcohol gives wine lighter weight and is usually more elegant and gentle.

Alcohol level is also a good indicator of sweetness. If the wine comes from a warm region but has lower alcohol, the wine is potentially a bit sweeter. A wine below about 10.5 per cent from anywhere in the world often indicates some level of sugar left over.

Furthermore, consider the alcohol level's suitability for what you plan on doing with the wine. Do you really want a 14.5 per cent monster wine if you're planning to share it with your grandma before going to the theatre? She'll be asleep before the curtain rises. If you have a chunk of beef that needs some power and body to balance it, though, 14.5 per cent sounds ideal!

Grape Varietals

Most wines display the grapes used to make it on the back label. Even the French are coming round to it. They are usually displayed as percentages, if it's a blend. As with alcohol percentage, take these with a pinch of salt. They'll be close, but it is not an exact science. Even a small percentage, five per cent say, of a particular grape in the mix can make quite a difference to a wine, especially if it's an aromatic or heavily tannic variety. If you see varieties with distinct characters you recognise, perhaps Muscat, Nebbiolo, Mourvèdre or similar, on the label, they'll add something significant even in small quantities.

Grapes are a great indication of the style of the wine. Especially combined with knowledge of the area's climate and the particular vintage.

Oak

Sometimes a back label talks about oak in detail. The name of the wine may even suggest oak, Ten Barrels Sauvignon would be a crap name but would do just that. However, it isn't always obvious from the label whether a wine has spent time in wood. Terms like Reserva, Gran Reserva, Reserve, etc. tend to indicate mature wines, usually oak aged. These terms are often protected and signify specific maturation times and oak use (with Rioja, for example), but be aware that for many regions these terms are unregulated and are just used by marketeers to indicate the style.

Bottled at . . .

The back label will tell you where the wine was bottled. It might simply say 'Produced By . . .' or a term such as *'mis en bouteille'*. If this is followed by the name of the winery or *'mis en bouteille au chateau'*, for example, then it was bottled on site at the winery. If it is a random number or obscure business address, it is likely that the wine was either shipped in bulk and bottled in the country you bought it, or made by a large volume contract producer for a branded wine. This doesn't indicate lower quality necessarily, but if it's coupled with a low price, it may be an indication that it's a wine designed to be a 'crowd pleaser', which often means a fair bit of sweetness and easy, simple, fruity character, rather than anything too challenging or explorative.

Sulphites

A wine containing more than 10mg sulphur per litre, used as a preservative, will always clearly state 'Contains Sulphites' in the language of the country in which it is sold. Check the back label. This is regulated by law. For more detail on the role and effects of sulphites, see the chapter on How Wine Is Made (page 22)

Vegetarian, Vegan, Allergens

Wine is swiftly getting up to speed with dietary information. Many wine labels now state whether they are vegetarian and vegan-friendly, but it is not universal or mandated by law at present.

If a bottle doesn't confirm either way, it may well use fining agents derived from animal sources. These, when used correctly, would not be present in the final wine but, irrespective, it is obviously important that everyone is aware and able to make conscious choices.

Similarly, there should be no allergens in wine that are not mentioned on the label. In December 2023 the EU passed the first major update to wine label legislation in decades. This includes a requirement to display all allergens and additives used throughout the winemaking process – greater transparency is coming.

Disgorgement Date (Sparkling)

Increasingly common, but not 'the norm', producers of traditional sparkling wine may put disgorgement dates on their back label. It may be subtly coded (for their own stock management purposes, but easily worked out by an eagle-eyed wino) or very prominently displayed for the consumer's benefit. They are interesting as this tells you how long the wine has been without the yeast, ageing on the cork. Too short a time (less than six months) and the wine may be best to leave for a while to settle and reach its peak. The greater the time since the wine was disgorged, the more complex, gently nutty and rich in texture the wine is likely to be.

Wine Colour

Not on the label, but if you can see the wine's colour through the bottle, you can tell a fair bit from that alone. Darker, honeyed whites will usually be more mature, often oaked examples. The darker a rosé, the more flavourful and rich it will usually be. More translucent, lighter-coloured reds tend to be more fresh and lighter in style. Although, as mentioned before, this is not always the case, especially if they are mature.

7.

Wine Lists

Someone on the table says, 'You like wine, you choose.' The walls come in. All eyes are on you. A sudden, pervading sense that your relationships, career, future are riding on this choice. A high-wire acrobatic trick is about to be performed. You're walking out of this to rapturous applause, or not walking out at all. I am an overthinker. I know, though, that this isn't an experience unique to me. Many people – the majority, I reckon – find wine lists daunting.

Wine lists are a necessary evil. Necessary because they are your gateway to choice and exploration. A warm glow, tipsiness, dancing. They are an opportunity for a little self-expression by the restaurant, which is what we're all here for, within reason. Evil because they're essentially long lists of data.

Understandably, most people decide the amount they want to spend and choose a wine just above or just below that.

There are ways to navigate these things, though. Ways to enjoy them, even. To embrace the opportunity they present. Here, by and large, is how they work and how to crack the code.

How Is this List Structured?

Sommeliers are forever trying to make their wine lists as accessible and easy to read as possible. They want you to find the gems, the perfect wine, with relative ease. They also want you to see the fun, off-the-beaten-track wines they have added, rather than just spotting the Provence rosé and having three of those.

So, there are myriad ways that wine lists are structured. Job one, get the measure of the list. Give it a cursory glance in full. Is it a classic sparkling, white, rosé, red with ascending prices? Bit boring, but easy to choose your price range. Maybe they've grouped wines into stylistic categories, 'Bold and Fruity', 'Crisp and Refreshing', etc. Easy to make a quick decision, if you know what you want style-wise. Less so, if you fancied looking across a wide range with exploration in mind.

Work out how the particular wine list in front of you functions before setting off. You may find that you gain an opinion quite quickly on how wine lists are best arranged. Like many things in wine, it's quite personal and everyone has an opinion.

Price: How it Works and How to Get the Best Value

As we all know, the general model for restaurants is that they have an enormous range of running costs and only one source of income to cover them: the menu. For this reason, plus the beautiful setting and service, you pay significantly more for the privilege of enjoying wine in a restaurant than at home. Likewise with the food. A bottle of wine at a typical restaurant costs you three-and-a-half times the price the restaurant paid for it. Totally fair enough.

Interestingly, diners are typically more price-conscious with wine lists than they are food menus. In some part, I think this is because we know food in restaurants benefits from an economy of scale that wine lists don't. I'll explain. Often, with a bit of effort, you could purchase the same bottle of wine from a wine merchant and drink it at home. Aside from the charm and grace of the waiter and someone else doing the washing up, you would, by and large, have the same experience for a lower price. It feels attainable. The food, not so much. If you did find the same butcher and bought a single steak, you would pay enormously more for that single steak than the restaurant did when they regularly order fifty of them. You couldn't buy the three single cloves of garlic, pinches of seasoning and single-portion quantities of the sides it came with. Your financial outlay to achieve the exact same dish at home would be huge, requiring you to have large quantities of lots of different ingredients paid for but left over, and not to mention the skill of a professional chef to pull it off. So, by that measure, the price you pay for a great dish in a restaurant is wildly justifiable compared to the wine.

The other reason we are price sensitive with wine lists is a lack of confidence in our own knowledge, our ability to make an informed choice. The easiest way to alleviate this is to chat to the waiters and sommeliers. Be upfront about your budget and seek their advice based on your preferences and menu choices.

There are good value spots to be found on all wine lists, listing the wines where the restaurant will have marked up the price slightly less than the standard. These tend to be the wines the restaurant wants you to try. Seek out off-the-beaten-track grapes, styles and countries. Perhaps there are wines from the same country as the restaurant's cuisine? Perhaps there are small-production, rarely exported wines the somme-lier found on a recent trip?

Conversely, the wines representing least value, often with the biggest markup, are the big names on campus – New Zealand sauvignon blanc, big name producers, Chablis, that sort of thing. The restaurant knows they are popular and will sell themselves, so they don't need to entice you with the pricing. Don't avoid these wines, necessarily, tuck in and have a whale of a time if you want, but purely in terms of pricing, they are rarely a steal.

Another tip is to choose wine-focussed restaurants. Those that have put equal emphasis on their wines and their food. There are increasing numbers of wine-destination restaurants, at all price points, where they intentionally work on lower markups, wanting guests to make the journey specifically to enjoy great wine at great value.

A really nice touch, for the consumer, is a concept known as 'cash margin', where restaurants eschew the traditional markup system (adding a percentage of the bottle's value) and add a standard value (perhaps £20 or £30) to each bottle's cost price. This incentivises customers to spend more on wine, as the greater the cost of the bottle, the better the value they get – due to the smaller proportionate of markup. I am an enormous fan of cash margin – it is often a key deciding factor in my choice of restaurant.

Generalise about Climate

This is back to the idea that wines from cooler climates are generally leaner and fresher in style than those from warm climates. The warmer the climate, the more bold, fruity and full-bodied the wine is likely to be. It isn't an exact science, but it rings true often enough to be an enormous help with a wine list. Use the information available to generalise about the climate of the region.

Wines by the Glass

I often advise people wanting to learn about wine to drink widely and variedly. Restaurants are a great opportunity to do this. Choose wines you haven't heard of, or have a clear reference for in your memory. Talking to the sommelier and ordering glass by glass is a great way to attain information.

Wines by the glass do not represent better or worse value for money than wines by the bottle, really. You may pay a small additional amount to drink by the glass, to compensate the restaurant for the risk of wastage involved in having the bottle open, but it will be tiny when compared to the convenience and opportunity to try a range of wines.

Speak to the Waiter

ALL experienced wine lovers take the sommelier's advice. In fact, the more you know, and the more confident and comfortable you feel, the more likely you will relinquish a little control and trust them.

A good waiter will know their wine list well. A sommelier will know it inside out and, contrary to some diners' concerns, they are there to help you find the right bottle for you. They are not there, unless they are supremely rubbish at their job, to upsell and push you into spending more.

When speaking to them, you want to establish a friendly rapport and be upfront about your budget. If you don't want to talk about specific wines, that's almost better, as it gives them more freedom to make suggestions. Tell them what you are eating. Try to articulate what wines you drink regularly or have enjoyed before; anything you dislike, too. They will be excited to cross reference these in their mind and come up with the right wine.

If you're friendly and chatty, they will often bring you samples of various wines to try. A lovely thing. Be honest about whether you like the samples; this isn't the same as when you've selected a bottle and sniff it to check it's corked. At that point, you're committed to the wine unless it's faulty. If the sommelier is offering samples, you can say 'That's not quite my thing' with abandon. Keep feedback as a personal perspective, rather than a critique, though. Wine is subjective and the sommelier will be very emotionally invested in any wines they show you. Don't break their heart!

Bin Ends

An odd term. You find it in wine shops, too, but often in restaurants. 'Bin Numbers' are the numbers denoting specific storage locations in a wine cellar. The cellar would be ordered chronologically by number. The wines on a large wine list are correspondingly numbered. Traditionally, and still often the case today, the waiter will use this 'Bin Number' to find the wine in the cellar. As the space in the cellar for that particular wine begins to empty, a restaurant may promote its 'Bin Ends', the last few bottles of that particular wine. Sometimes they represent great value, as the restaurant wants to sell them quickly to make room for the next wine.

8.

How to Choose Wine in a Shop

Floor to ceiling shelves, fully stacked with bottles. We're back in data overload territory. Whether you're dashing in on the way to a party or have a little weekend afternoon time to mull your way about, there are simply too many bottles to catalogue mentally and make a well-rounded decision. So, you need to break it up a bit.

How is the shop arranged? Easy regional categories? Styles of wine? Before anything, get the lay of the land, so you know which sections you want to investigate further.

Within your chosen sections, you're going to have to use your gut instinct to whittle them down. Their labels should speak to their individual character. You will find yourself drawn to labels that evoke the style of wine you are after, or occasion you are buying for. Let this do the initial heavy lifting, then look at those that leap out at you in more detail. Use the skills you've picked up in How to Read a Wine Label (pages 110–122) to gain insight into the wine from the label.

Seek the Experience of the Team

Much like a sommelier helping to navigate a wine list in a restaurant, there is enormous benefit in having a chat with the team in the shop. They know their range and will be excited to recommend wines to you. The joy of tasting and chatting about wine is literally why they do their job. They're often even geekier than sommeliers.

Take the same tack as when talking to a sommelier; get in early doors with a price range, to help refine their suggestions. Articulate the scenario in which you plan to drink the wine. Is it foodie, an aperitif, on the beach? Any references to wines you have enjoyed before, or grape varieties will help.

Try to avoid feeling committed to a wine if the team suggest it but you're unsure. Be polite about their recommendations, but don't feel pressured to walk out with something you aren't completely satisfied with.

Obviously, this is only really possible in an independent merchant. It'd be nigh on impossible in a supermarket.

Price: How it Works in Shops

Unless you are a premiership footballer, price will be a consideration in your wine shopping. So, always have an idea of what you want to spend before going into the shop and try to stick to it. That said, on occasion, as and when you can, do stretch your wine budget a little. A few extra pounds can give you access to new styles and regions that you haven't tried before, and exploration is the whole point.

Wine shops tend to sell wines for about one-and-a-half times the cost to them, so they represent fantastic value compared to restaurants. It's a different model – their overheads are smaller (but by no means small!), you are not drinking the wine on site. For all these reasons and more, they can work to a lower markup. It means the same wine sold by a producer at £10 (including taxes) would sit on a shop shelf at £15, but would be £35 in a restaurant.

Be savvy about discounts and deals. Many represent fantastic value and an opportunity to genuinely try wines that would usually be outside your price bracket. Supermarkets are especially strong at regular, seasonal wine offers. There are some pitfalls to avoid, though. Fake discounting is rife on big-brand, commercial wines in supermarkets. Be conscious of how often you see a particular wine on offer. If it is very regularly sold at a 'discount', then it has a falsely inflated standard price and the discount price isn't a discount at all; it's just what it should be. Avoid.

The True Value in a Bottle

When you buy a bottle of wine in a shop, there is about £1 worth of fixed transport and dry goods costs (bottles, labels, corks, etc.), sometimes much more. There is also usually some sort of alcohol duty added as a tax. These flex wildly depending on where in the world you are buying your wine. UK duty on a 12 per cent ABV 750ml bottle of still wine is £2.68, at the time of writing. Norway's equivalent is 44.55kr (roughly £3.29). France's is €0.04 (£0.03). Then there is the retailer and importer profit margin. Let's call that forty-five per cent combined, but it could be anywhere between thirty-five and sixty per cent. VAT or other sales tax will be added on top. This is often around twenty per cent but, again, varies by country. All this before we have even considered the price of the actual liquid in the bottle. Taking the examples above, in a £7 bottle of wine on the shelf in a UK supermarket, the wine itself is worth about £0.35. Which doesn't sound great, does it?

The good news is that those fixed costs of logistics, dry goods and duty remain the same, irrespective of the wine's sales value. So, when you spend £10 on a bottle of wine, the value of the wine leaps to around £2.05. The value grows exponentially from there. Buying a £15 bottle nets you approximately £4.95 worth of actual wine. By the time you spend £25, you're on for £10.75 worth of wine. My fag packet maths doesn't take into account marketing costs and makes some major guesstimates, but it's a pretty decent representation of the value of wine in your bottle. It pays to spend a little more, when possible.

Own Labels

There has been a proliferation of own-brand wines in supermarkets in recent years. I am often asked whether they are routinely awful or might actually be worth a punt. Of course, there are some better and worse cases but, on the whole, I think they are great examples of their type and a good way to broaden your tasting experience. They tend to sit in the more affordable price bracket, but in recent years supermarkets have introduced more premium wines, too. Across the price spectrum, they are usually solid examples of the wines they are and tend to be priced competitively. So, supermarket own-brand Soave will taste like a typical Soave should. It is in the supermarket's interest to ensure they are benchmark examples of the wine type. They may not offer the personality and uniqueness of a wine producer's core range, and they may not carry the 'wow' factor that makes a bottle suitable as a gift to take to a swanky party, but they will give you some insight into what that style of wine tastes like. So don't avoid them!

Shop Window Wines

Huge no-no! Don't buy wine that has been sitting in the shop window in direct sunlight. Find a bottle that has been as shaded as possible. We discussed the problems caused by UV light previously, and never is this more of an issue than in wine that has been stored badly in a wine shop window.

A very loose, illustrated timeline of the history of wine: tracking where and when (to the best of our knowledge) wine culture sprang up

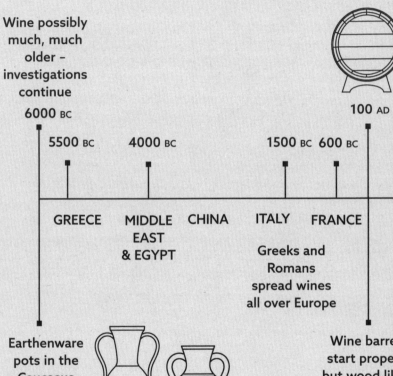

Wine possibly much, much older – investigations continue

6000 BC

5500 BC

4000 BC

1500 BC

600 BC

100 AD

GREECE

MIDDLE EAST & EGYPT

CHINA

ITALY

FRANCE

Greeks and Romans spread wines all over Europe

Earthenware pots in the Caucasus Mountains, modern-day Georgia

Wine barrel start proper but wood like used for 1,00 years prior

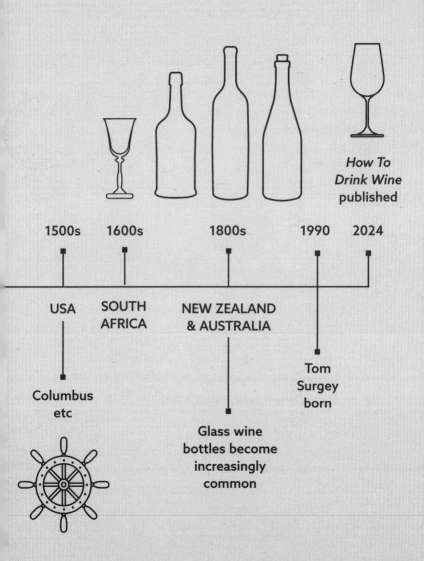

1500s 1600s 1800s 1990 2024

How To Drink Wine published

USA SOUTH AFRICA NEW ZEALAND & AUSTRALIA

Columbus etc

Glass wine bottles become increasingly common

Tom Surgey born

9.

Hangovers

The career path of a 'wine expert' is, unsurprisingly, fraught with hangovers. In fact, it is almost impossible to become one without having achieved a similar degree of expertise in the other. I am sure some rare individuals, pillars of Herculean self-control, do exist, but I am yet to meet one. So, I hope this is a useful little guide to the flip side of the coin.

Most studies suggest that almost everybody who overindulges in alcohol experiences hangovers. We all know someone who claims never to suffer from them but I am dubious of these claims. However, there are definitely quite dramatic differences in the speed with which certain individuals process alcohol. This may be why some people wake the next day feeling chipper while you feel as though you wrestled a buffalo and replaced your entire body's fluid with a swirling vortex of frogspawn. Outside of this natural diversity in how fast we break down alcohol in our liver, the key contributing factor to how dreadful we feel the next day is likely to be our hydration level. Ethanol is a diuretic; it makes you pee a lot. Dehydration sets in quickly when drinking alcohol. My biggest tip at wine tastings, even when spitting, is drink as much water as you can.

As well as the issue of ethanol-induced dehydration, congeners (naturally occurring flavour and colour compounds) in wine are known to cause vasodilation, widening of the blood vessels, which can cause headaches. Adding further fuel to the fire are histamines, which are naturally present to a greater or lesser extent in fermented products. Histamines can cause headaches, too, and all sorts of hay-fever-like symptoms.

This trio of culprits may be the most likely causes of your hangover, but there are a myriad of other contributing compounds that are sticking the boot in, too. The truth is, you've overdone it and now you're paying the price. But, what can you do to soften the blow?

Prevention

Water is key. Both while you're out and about doing the drinking, and after. A pint of the stuff before bed, another by your bedside for during the night, and maybe a back-up pint for first thing in the morning.

The next best thing is pacing yourself. I am certainly not going to lecture anyone on this. It takes a bit of practise. The path to finding your own balance is littered with mistakes, hopefully none too awful. Speedy drinking will exacerbate your hangover dramatically, so ideally you want to keep a steady pace and give your body a chance to break down some of the alcohol as you go. If you keep the pace calm, you can often escape even the slightest hint of a hangover, even after a lovely, long day of social wine sharing with friends.

Eat. Every parent forever has warned their teenagers of the perils of drinking on an empty stomach. With good reason, too. Eating before and at intervals while you drink helps to slow the absorption of alcohol into your blood stream. As your body processes the alcohol at a slow but steady rate, the food provides a welcome delay to the new alcohol you're adding to your system.

There are plenty of myths and untruths related to hangovers that persist. In fact, some of us, have our own suspicions about what the usual suspects are that cause us particular issue. I have a thing about sugary sweet drinks – I am convinced they make my hangovers appalling. Port and deep, rich red wines may cause a little extra pain, as they contain higher quantities of those pesky congeners than whites, but surely not enough to avoid choosing them if you fancy a glass. Sulphites get some stick, too; they can make you feel tight chested if you really overdo it. But it's unlikely that they contribute to your common or garden hangover symptoms unless you have an allergy. The old mantra of 'Beer before wine, always fine; wine before beer, oh dear' doesn't hold water, in my experience. In fact, the entire wine trade is partial to a cleansing ale after a long day of tasting wines. Sometimes it's the only thing that will do.

Cure

Water! Rehydration is your quickest, easiest route back to feeling semi-human. This may need to be in the form of a Lucozade Orange, if you're feeling particularly beastly.

Vitamins and nutrients. Famously a good thing. Alcohol removes them really quickly from your system. Especially zinc and vitamin B. So, if you want to be really belt and braces, replacing these by eating nutrient-rich foods or taking high-quality multivitamins *might* help. As might a Virgin Mary.

Hair of the dog. While often an attractive proposition, it only really delays the hangover, I am advised to say. It is to be attempted only when a 'kill or cure' policy needs to be adopted.

One day, should you wish, we can sit by the fire and I will regale you with the highlights of the combined weeks and months of my life that I have spent hungover. The worst were truly appalling and so much greater than just physical discomfort. The anxiety and existential dread and worry they conjure can be truly awful. By your thirties, that anxiety can last all week. It isn't worth it. Your best bet is to follow the advice above and pace yourself. I'm done with hangovers – they suck.

10.

On Drinking
Wine in 2024

If you see it how I see it (and I hope, having read this book, you might), wine is everything. Every potential aspect and fleeting nuance of nature and the human condition is contained in a single, delicious glass. It's vital. An invitation to be in the moment. A catalyst for reflection. A rare giver of space to allow your imagination and ideas room to play around in an otherwise chaotic, rushed modern life. A social elixir offering a shared, communal experience, where everyone has a unique, subjective, sensory encounter at the same time.

The drinking of it, the ritual of choosing and buying and coveting and opening and swirling and taking a moment and sniffing it. The thinking and maybe the occasional reading about it. Analogue moments in a whirlwind of digitally pumped opinion, social media gurus, deadlines, moral responsibility. Egregiously opulent. A laughably frivolous thing to occupy your mind, your hand, your tummy. A purely pleasurable thing. You should be chuffed to bits with yourself.

Somewhat counter-intuitively, for a person in my position, I will be forever grateful for the health warnings and awareness around alcohol that fill the modern narrative. Not only is it clearly positive to be aware and make conscious choices around our lifestyle to ensure personal and societal well-being, but access to well-researched and freely available advice on how to live a healthy, balanced life is one of the great democratic successes of our time. I'm a huge advocate for eating well and looking after yourself, whatever that means for you. But, equally importantly, this awareness of our responsibilities when consuming alcohol brings a naughtiness and sense of misadventure to the occasions when we choose to raise a glass together, which is such a delicious sensation in and of itself, isn't it?! I love it. The raised eyebrow accompanied by an invitation to have a cheeky glass of wine. We so rarely get to feel naughty. The shared complicity in doing something as outrageously opulent as opening a bottle of fizz. Imagine! The audacity! These are social cues and moments that bring us together. Regularly enjoying wine in 2024 is like walking a tightrope. Moreish and compelling, an endlessly attractive idea; it's essential you are aware of what balance means to you, but it's equally important to allow yourself to fly a little too close to the sun with some regularity. Seek joyful moments and embrace the opportunity when it comes to indulge. Please don't wait for special occasions; liberally season everyday life with delicious sips of consciously chosen wines.

Equally, enjoy the considered moments when you choose not to drink wine. Anticipation is half the fun and, like anything, without pauses in the enjoyment, wine becomes a mundane and ordinary experience . . . It's paramount that you don't lose the sparkle. Plus, it's highly addictive and very bad for you in large volumes, so give it some respect, yeah?

Note to editor: a masterclass in balance there, don't you agree, George?

11.

Forget All Else –
Ten Key Wine Facts

1 Wine is made from grapes.

2 Wine carries a sense of place. This is called terroir.

3 Wine tasting is very subjective. Your experience is true to you.

4 There are approximately 10,000 wine grape varieties; of which approximately 1,500 are used commercially.

5 Wine has been produced for at least 8,000 years. The earliest known evidence of winemaking comes from around Georgia.

6 The largest-by-volume wine-producing countries are Italy, Spain and France, but wine is made all over the world.

7 Most whites should be served just above fridge temperature and most reds just below room temperature.

8 When storing wine, keep it lying on its side at a constant temperature below 22°C and out of sunlight.

9 Corks DO NOT mean the wine is better than those with screw caps.

10 The best value is found 'off the beaten track'. Explore the wine world.

12.

Wine Recommendations to Start You Down the Path

I want this book to be an easy-to-digest, catch-all guide, providing everything you need to get really stuck into wine. As such, of course, I want to recommend some wines for you. Split into key different styles, these are wines with which to begin your journey. If you like one style of wine, but haven't found your way into others, these are your gateway wines; a selection of grapes and wine types to give you a thorough lay of the land, from which you can then stray beyond and explore further.

For each wine style, I recommend five easy-to-find wines. Having these five in your consciousness gives you a very solid base to feel you really 'get' that type of wine. They will form your initial frame of reference, giving you context when tasting other wines. For each style, I've also thrown in a few esoteric wines that might provide a bit of fun to explore further if you can find them.

Of course, this cannot be an exhaustive list. They are simply a gentle nudge from me to set you off down a joyful road of vinous discovery. I also want this book to remain relevant for many years, so you can reference it as you require. This restricts me from recommending specific wines. They would be out of date before the pages were printed. So, you'll need to use the skills picked up in the earlier chapters to choose specific examples of these recommended wine types.

Wine Without Food

Sometimes you just want a glass of wine. You don't need food. Here are great wines to drink with friends on sunny weekend afternoons, to sip when cooking at home in your kitchen, or whenever, frankly.

The best wines to be enjoyed on their own are approachable and delicious, which means low in tannin and bitterness if they're red. They should be mouthwatering, with crunchy, bright character, not austere. Juicy, fruitful wines. If they have a little extra 'something', a little mineral layer, a subtle herbaceous finish, something that keeps you intrigued, then even better.

English Sparkling Rosé

Sparkling rosé is often maligned by the pros. There are some great examples made the world over, but it can be a bit clunky and feel like an afterthought – a commercially driven product, rather than something made because it is extraordinary. English sparkling rosé, however, generally bucks this trend. The typically longer, colder growing season than in Champagne or the many other Traditional Method wine regions, achieves a concentration and intensity of tart red berry fruit like no other. English rosé is bright, high energy, with really defined varietal fruit flavours. Seek out Traditional Method examples with at least a few years' lees ageing in bottle. Worth every penny.

Soave

Just one of a host of epic, indigenous, regional Italian white wines that could happily sit here. Soave is produced from the zingy, citrus, peach and melon-scented Garganega grape. Try Soave at all price points but, once in a while, seek out pricier examples from the Soave Classico Superiore DOCG traditional vineyard area for extra depth and concentration. Like many great regional Italian whites, look out for a subtle and pleasant almond nuttiness right on the tip of the finish.

New Zealand Sauvignon Blanc

Everyone's mum's favourite. Such a big name on campus, it feels silly recommending NZ Sauv. It's ubiquity, though, is due to its extraordinary combination of bright, ripe, tropical fruits dialled up to eleven, alongside equally punchy, mouthwatering acidity. The best have elegant, herbal, mineral notes within the fruit-salad explosion. Just epically yummy. Great on their own and a total crowd pleaser. Try other Sauvignon Blanc examples, like Chilean, South African and French, to get a feel for the spectrum of styles this aromatic variety can achieve.

Cooler-climate Grenache Red (Garnacha Tinto)

Oh, cooler-climate, crunchy, perfumed Grenache, how I love you. Sometimes referred to as the poor man's Pinot Noir, for its similar, elegant acidity, medium body and fine, cherry, berry fruit character. It can be rugged and dense when oak aged and blended with other varieties in regions like Spain's Priorat. But we're not talking about Priorat, as nice as it can be. Seek out Grenache grown high up hillsides with those Wild Boar roaming free or grown on breezy coastlines. The Iberian Peninsula – particularly northwest Spain is a great place to start but you can find these in Australia, New Zealand, increasingly everywhere! And beware cheap Grenache from hot climates, which can present like an insipid, boozy, strawberry jam.

Beaujolais

Not the thin, nouveau, faddy stuff. Like shoulder pads, spandex and perms, that might be fun for a night, but only your dad wants it back properly. Beaujolais is proper, elegant, complex, lighter-bodied red wine made from Gamay grapes and is perfect pre-dinner or for drinks with friends. We're in cherries and berries territory again, this time with subtle, earthy, savoury spice and sometimes a bit of pencil-shavings piquancy thrown in. Embrace the complex layers, while revelling in the easy-drinking fruity notes. Look for the often-great-value 'Beaujolais Village', slightly upper-tier quality wines, or wines from specific 'crus', ten defined areas around key villages offering more depth, richness and terroir specificity.

Once you've tried these, seek out some more esoteric, easy-drinking wonders: Cap Classique, South Africa's Traditional Method sparkling wines; Kidonitsa, from Monemvasia, Greece; other Italian regional white grapes, like Cortese, Fiano, Falanghina and Pecorino (not the cheese!); and Romanian Pinot Noir.

Fresh, Clean Whites

We're talking dream seafood wines here. Racy, refreshing acidity. Wine of clarity and rejuvenating energy. Bracing, like jumping in a cold pool on a hot day. Tense, lean citruses are the order of the day, flavour wise, joined by a stoney, sometimes salty tang in many of the best examples. Oak will be minimal, if there at all.

You want to be looking at cooler-climate regions in general. Cold countries. Higher altitude in warmer countries. Windswept islands and vineyards clinging to rugged coastlines.

Shellfish, grilled fish, fish and chips, these wines will nail anything that comes out of the sea (excluding condoms and shopping trolleys). Beyond that, these will cut through fatty dishes and zing hard against salt, so use them as a foil to pork belly, fried chicken, that sort of business. All day, mate.

Albariño

Is there a more trendy grape variety? Probably not. Whether electric and bright in its homeland of Rías Baixas, Galicia, or just south, over the Minho into northern Portugal as gently herbaceous but equally fine Alvarinho (doing the heavy lifting for the epic Vinho Verde wines), Albariño is a dry white superstar. It ages well, the palate getting richer and the fruit maturing into greater depth, but we mostly drink it fresh and youthful. Tense tropicals, citrus and peach, subtle saltiness.

It's such a dream. Try riper, fuller examples from New Zealand and South Africa, too.

Cool-climate Chardonnay

Think classics, like Chablis and Champagne, but also high-altitude, mountainous regions, such as the Italian Alps and South Africa's great mountain ranges. Chardonnay produces a wide spectrum of wines, from super-racy to bold and rich. The best, cool-climate, lean Chardonnay styles have fine acidity, subtle, green orchard and citrus fruit character. They may or may not have oak ageing involved. Chablis which is usually unoaked, suddenly becomes an oaked wine in the top-most Grand Cru wines . . . while this adds weight and creamy texture, they can still be very elegant and fresh in their younger years.

Assyrtiko

Grown across Greece, with its home being windswept, volcanic Santorini, Assyrtiko is now being planted elsewhere in the world. Ultra-fresh, lemon-lime citrus and often salty sea air characters are key. Assyrtiko has an extraordinary ability to get nicely ripe in the sunshine and still retain huge levels of acidity. It can be oaked, but most examples tend not to be, or only very slightly. It ages beautifully. Expect to see more Assyrtiko in your shopping basket in years to come. Get on board now!

Clare Valley Riesling

We could pick epic dry and off-dry Riesling from anywhere, like Germany's classic Mosel and Rheinegau regions, or Austria's truly elegant examples, but for pure freshness and mouthwatering zest, Australia's Clare Valley is a great shout. Bone-dry and tasting like a freshly squeezed lime, it has Riesling's trademark subtle, waxy, floral, aromatic character. They age outrageously, too, getting waxier and potentially gaining a little hint of petrol over a long time, but young they are a dream, cool, crisp white. See other areas in Australia, too, such as the nearby Eden Valley, for similarly top-notch Riesling.

Grüner Veltliner

Another trendy grape varietal we can expect to see more of, 'Grüner' is Austria's iconic white grape. It also grows across a swathe of Eastern Europe, such as in Hungary and Slovakia. Lime and green apple and a distinctive white pepper spice is the classic combo. The finesse and freshness of Riesling, with less waxy aromatics. Typically unoaked. Look at examples from Austria's Wachau and Kremstal or southern Burgenland for a range of regional styles on the same zingy, subtly spiced theme.

Some esoteric zingers for you to try: Donzelinho Branco, a rare, fresh native of Douro Valley, Portugal; Nascetta, an almost extinct, aromatic but super-fresh white from Piedmont, Italy; and Godello, a fine, minerally, intense, high-quality white from Spain's Galicia region.

Rich, Full Whites

The fatter end of the wedge. Chunky, robust white wines. Snuggly hugs in a glass. Honey and fresh baked bread and ripe melon. Opulent and outrageous and satisfying. The best are held in place with a clean line of uplifting acidity; you need this to give structure to the opulent beasts.

Hunt these bad boys in warmer climates. You'll typically find them languishing on sunny plains and on lower mountains slopes in full afternoon sun. Winemakers often lean into this natural opulence by giving them time in oak barrels or having the lees (yeast) stirred repeatedly as the wine matures, adding depth and creamy texture.

These are food-pairing legends – white, meatier fish dishes, like turbot; roast chicken; pork; and rich, white-bean stews. These are the dauphinois potato of the wine world. Oh, mama.

Oaked Chardonnay

The main player in the world of full-bodied white wines. Every major country has a version. From the quintessential and diverse spectrum of more-or-less-buttery, hazel-nut-styled Chardonnay found in Burgundy, to full-throttle, vanilla- and popcorn-powerhouse Californians and everything in between. Chardonnay is epic. Look for medium to warm climates, which give extra weight and power to the Chardonnay itself, then check for use of oak to add further spice, texture and creaminess. The price range here can be enormous, from the cheapest to the most expensive wines in the world. Try a range. And try to get someone else to fork out for the Meursault. . .

Dry, Old Vine Chenin Blanc

One of the most purely joyful, thought-provoking wines available. Young Chenin can be lean and zingy. Old vines (not a set age, but maybe twenty years plus) give increasing concentration, complexity and intensity of flavour in the right hands. Often oaked, sometimes blended with other varieties, expect lemon peel, subtle, baked-orchard fruits and buckets of cream and honey with a fine, fresh acidity cleaning it up. France's Loire is its home and makes very diverse styles from sweet to dry, but full-bodied, dry, Old Vine Chenin has reached new heights in South Africa, so start there, no question.

Grenache Blanc (Garnacha Blanca)

I am such a Grenache fanboy, it's embarrassing. Having
eulogised about crunchy, lighter Grenache reds, I'd throw them
out the window immediately if I was forced to pick between
them and their rarer, white grape sibling, Grenache Blanc.
Powerhouse wines with a big frame – the best styles have a
tight core (much like your author, ahem). Grenache Blanc's
flavours are subtle – ripe, baked citrus and green fruits sort
of thing – but it's their firm structure, often warm alcohol and
honeyed, rich layers that make the best examples so appealing.
Search France's Roussillon and southern Rhône, as well as
South Africa. It's sometimes found giving structure to blends
with more aromatic, flavourful varieties.

Viognier and Rhône Blends

Perfumed, rich, opulent Viognier. Orange blossom, honeysuckle, apricots. This is not a shy, retiring varietal. Most at
home in the northern Rhône Valley in France, Viognier has
made a big comeback in recent decades, now being planted
in warm climates the world over. It's sometimes blended with
northern Rhône cool-cats Marsanne (big-boned, honeysuckle)
and Roussanne (herbal, floral). USA, Australia and South Africa
are making interesting moves with these grapes, too.

Semillon

Often a rich, fuller-bodied blending partner to the more
aromatic and zingy Sauvignon in Bordeaux's dry and very
sweet white wines (like Sauternes), Semillon crops up as a
solo varietal on occasion. Australia is a big fan, especially in
the Hunter Valley where long bottle-aged examples can be
extraordinarily aromatic. Semillon is sometimes oaked, but not
always. If not too ripe, it can retain some quite Sauvignon-like

aromas. You may see Sauvignon/Semillon blends from around the world; they will usually be fuller bodied, slightly softer wines by comparison to pure Sauvignon.

Some off-the-beaten track, full-bodied whites for you to explore: Timorasso, Piedmont; Marsanne and Roussanne Rhône blends without Viognier; and Gros Manseng from Jurançon, France.

Rosé and Orange Wines

Basically, these are skin-contact wines that haven't gone the whole distance and become a red. Rosé and orange wines span a spectrum, from swimming-pool quaffers, fascinating, complex foodie gems, and intense, grippy, intellectually challenging rarities.

These wines are made in every climate, in every country of the world. They follow the usual principle of warmer regions producing riper, more flavourful wines, but this is mitigated enormously by the amount of time the skins are left in touch with the pressed grape juice as it ferments. Provence's pale, elegant rosés don't necessarily match up to expectations of the style produced in a warm, Mediterranean region, for example. Earlier picking to retain acidity and very minor skin contact can give an unexpected freshness.

For such a diverse range of wines, they are easily categorised as one of the best, most complimentary food-pairing styles of wine available. The best have the acidity of a white balanced by greater texture and richness. Having less tannic bitterness and intensity than a red means they sit bang in the middle style-wise and, impressively, can go with almost anything from classic brasserie dishes to Asian-inspired spice.

The more aromatic, floral wines in the category (often light orange wines) and the more rugged, heavily tannic wines (usually darker, amber wines) are a little more specific, pairing best with light, crispy, salty nibbles and more substantial, grilled meats and vegetables, respectively.

With a decent dose of fashion and prevailing consumer trends dictating that the paler the rosé, the better it is, it's important to remember that those of us who are interested in wine push ourselves beyond this boundary. There is a wealth of skin-contact wines out there to explore in every conceivable shade. We'll all be drinking darker rosé in a decade's time, I guarantee it.

Provence Rosé and Other Pale Pinks

The homeland of so-pale-they're-nearly-white rosé is France's Provence. It has built a lifestyle brand around its excellent wines, evoking Saint-Tropez and Mediterranean glamour. Made with minor skin contact prior to fermentation, expect medium acidity and light, elegant, red berry and citrus notes. Very pale rosé is now made the world over, alternative examples often have greater depth of flavour and complexity than Provence at half the price. Look at France's Provence-hugging southern Rhône and Languedoc, Greece (where the local variety Agiorgitiko can make amazing pale rosé), and England. Options are widespread and available to explore!

Deep Pink Rosé

Rosé with more skin contact, sometimes even a little during fermentation. This properly pink style is sometimes oak aged for added complexity. Southern Rhône's Tavel is a classic, as are those from nearby Bandol and Spain's Rioja. Deeper, more flavourful rosé, they sometimes display a little extra texture from subtle tannin. In some countries, Greece for example, leaving them off-dry is common. These can be hugely refreshing as an aperitif and with a wide range of foods.

Dark Rosé

Is that a light red? Maybe. It's bloody close. Who cares? Treat it like a rosé, just with loads more flavour. Increasingly, producers around the world, from Languedoc in France to Central Otago in New Zealand, are producing very, VERY dark rosés from grapes as diverse as Pinot Noir and Cinsault, by simply giving them longer skin contact than typical rosé, but still less than a red. Flavourful, brilliant partners for lighter dishes, they tend to have low tannins, medium acidity and bright, crunchy character. You'll know them when you spot them; get to a sunny picnic situation asap!

Light Orange Wine

These are the gateway wines to orange as a category. Always made with local varieties and, as such, very diverse. They regularly include a floral, aromatic variety, like Muscat, in a blend, alongside something that brings some weight to give pretty, welcoming charm to the wine. Be it Fiano and Falanghina in Italy, or Sauvignon, Riesling, Chenin Blanc, you name it, these are wines with anything from a few days to a week or so's skin contact time, during the fermentation. Not long enough to become tannic and bitter, just enough to gain some extra grip and depth of flavour. They will be somewhere between a slightly golden white wine and bright, honey in colour.

Deeper Amber Wines

A more specialist style – not something you tend to find in supermarkets. Often very premium pricing, this is an important historical wine style in Georgia and far northeast Italy's Collio region, as well as on the neighbouring Slovenian border. Habitually made using indigenous grapes, like thick-skinned Ribolla Gialla, these are orange wines aged for potentially years on their skins. Often aged in clay amphora buried in the ground, to keep the skins and wine in a gentle, perpetual momentum, they are usually dry, deeply flavoured with baked fruits, mature floral notes, earthy spices and a push-pull of racy acidity and intense tannin. Divisive in their style, they are an important reference point for those wanting to feel they know the full spectrum of orange wines.

What are the next steps in the search for rosé and orange esoterica? You can get lost in orange and amber wines for many happy years, tasting and exploring the breadth the category has to offer. Also, try more mature rosés. We are routinely told rosé is a young drinking style, which is not always the case; the less common, oak-aged, more premium rosés from Provence, Rioja and other parts of the world can gain amazing complexity after many years of bottle age.

Light Reds

In general, I think people veer towards riper, more full-bodied red wines. I think their intense flavour, sometimes sweet, fruity character and sensation of tannic power gives the impression they are delivering 'more' to the drinker. Lighter styles, counter-intuitively perhaps, sometimes take a little more effort to get into. Less bombastic and in-your-face, these are thoughtful, sometimes delicate styles with a slimmer profile.

This is the playing field for thinner-skinned black grape varieties. Often those with more perfume, more crunchy, juicy berry and cherry fruits. There is suddenly the potential to chill them down a touch. They make up for their lack of clout with a focus on elegance and subtle, nuanced layers of aroma. Long-lingering, mineral or herb-scented finishes.

Climatically, these often come from cooler, medium-temperature areas, but it isn't so straightforward. The natural wine movement and general trend for minimal intervention winemaking has fostered the development of lighter-bodied wines from what are often traditionally quite beefy grapes. This happens through less skin contact and extractive processing in the winery.

Food wise, we're talking game birds, venison and lighter red meats, lamb, that sort of thing. They can be great choices for cheeses, especially those wines with bright acidity and fresh, juicy fruit. The same goes for Italian tomato-based dishes. A little chill in the fridge for half an hour before serving often helps them immensely.

Pinot Noir

The poster-boy for lighter-bodied reds. Although, Pinot Noir can get quite tannic and robust in certain areas of Burgundy, so it presents a spectrum but is always on a slighter frame than most. In warmer regions, expect silky smooth, juicy black fruits and subtle baking spices. In cooler climates, expect more tightly structured, acid-held red and black berry fruits with subtle, earthy, musky perfume. Pinot Noir produces some of the most highly sought-after red wines in the world, typically in Burgundy. Oak ageing adds some muscle to it and it has the potential to age for a long time. Dip your toes into a variety of areas of Burgundy when budget allows, lower-price-point Pinot Noir from Chile and Romania offers good value and more accessible, easy-drinking styles. The USA, especially coastal California, offers extraordinarily expressive, classy, often obviously oaked styles to explore, too.

Gamay

The historically underappreciated black grape of Beaujolais. Thin skinned, like Pinot Noir, when it is at its best it makes remarkably similar wines to Pinot Noir; bright berry fruited, light tannin, perfumed spices, a little pepper sometimes. It often represents great value compared to Burgundian Pinot Noir, as Beaujolais is Burgundy's neighbour immediately south. Wines displaying the 'Beaujolais Village' level of quality are usually great value, as this denotes some of the better vineyards in Beaujolais. The 'Crus' themselves – ten villages with the best sites in Beaujolais – are the top of the tree, quality-wise, and are still much more accessibly priced than top Burgundy!

Corvina

Sour cherries lead a bright, juicy welcome in this delicious, easy-drinking wine. Corvina is the star black grape in the red blends of Italy's Lake Garda region, Bardolino, and further northeast in Veneto under the name Valpolicella. Sometimes dried and intensified to make higher-alcohol, heavier Amarone, as a straightforward, traditional wine, it makes tinglingly acidic, refreshing, perfect lunchtime red wines. Increasingly bottled as a single varietal, it is joyful and moreish, and ever such great value in an Italian restaurant.

Cabernet Franc

The unsung single-varietal red wine hero of France's Loire Valley and important blending component in classic Bordeaux. Cabernet Franc makes medium-bodied, herby, leafy, aromatic red wines with black- and red-berry fruit flavours and fine acidity. They are great for drinking young, but can mature for a few years and gain extra complexity. Like Gamay, they can sometimes have a little pencil-shavings note in there. Fun, expressive, complex wines on a fine frame.

Lower extraction, 'natural' styles

The trend for winemakers to be less hands-on in the winery is driving a revolution in less heavily extracted (pressed, stirred, punched-down skins during fermentation and maturation to gain extra weight and flavour) red wines the world over. Great examples come from Portugal, where producers are taking traditionally dense, tannic grapes like Baga or Douro Valley Port varieties and producing lighter, more perfumed, 'smashable' styles. Also look to South Africa, Australia, France, all over. In general, I am a fan. Seek red wines that are relatively transparent in the bottle, rather than fully translucent, often with funky, modern labelling.

Other lighter red styles to explore: Alfrocheiro, Portugal; Blaufränkisch, Austria (although some can be fuller in style); Grenache from cooler-climate sites; and Frappato, Sicily.

Heavy Reds

More common than light, fresh reds; bold, flavourful, weighty reds are a highly revered category of wine the world over. Often seen as the pinnacle of wine's potential.

Regularly requiring a fair amount of sunshine and warmth to ripen sufficiently, the grape varieties best suited to these styles are often at their most expressive when there is 'just enough' sunshine, rather than an abundance, which can lead to them being brash and overly alcoholic. Many of the wines are bolstered further with oak ageing, often in new barrels giving pronounced vanilla and luxurious, velvety textures to well-ripened fruit.

Food-wise, we're certainly in the big protein segment of the menu – red meats, high-protein bean-based dishes. We're talking cuts of beef with well-marbled fat, seared over fire, long-roasted, caramelised vegetables – foods with equally intense, rich flavours to stand up to the wine.

Cabernet Sauvignon

One of the most widely planted grape varieties in the world. The poster-boy for powerhouse, intensely flavoured red wines the world over. Deeply coloured, highly tannic wines with tense acidity. Blackcurrants, green leaf and cedar are common tasting notes, sometimes menthol. At its best it makes statuesque, silky, powerful reds, suitable for long ageing. Often oaked, adding vanilla and spice to the already big aromatic profile. Blended with Merlot and other varieties in Bordeaux and worldwide.

Syrah/Shiraz

Black pepper spice is Syrah's calling card. One of the more rich, rugged, brooding black grape varieties in wide availability. Black berry fruits and a rich, weighty mid-palate. It needs warm sun to ripen, but in relatively cooler sites (northern Rhône, France), it carries itself with an elegance and ethereal perfume that it loses in warmer locations. Widely planted in Australia as Shiraz, where it regularly achieves richer, riper, juicier fruit and higher alcohol, still with some dark fruit and spice. Often blended, it is used as a component to add structure and depth. Frequently oaked.

Malbec

Originally from Cahors in France under the name Cot, Malbec achieved international superstardom when it arrived in Argentina's high-altitude Mendoza region in the late 1800s. In Argentina, Malbec achieves a luscious, silky texture. Ripe, round palate filled with black berries and milk chocolate smoothness. Some examples, especially when oaked, can be complex and fine, worthy of many years' ageing. Many are bold, ripe, early drinkers with present but chewy, soft tannins. Such a crowd pleaser.

Merlot

Once in a while you find a Merlot that is exquisite. Cigar-box spice, perfectly ripe cocoa-dusted plums, liquid silk tannin. Quality oak helps. The majority can be a bit boring though; medium-full body, medium tannin, medium acidity, medium flavour intensity. Dial M for Medium. It's a popular variety, though, and one that should be firmly in your frame of reference. Widely planted, for me the best examples are Right Bank Bordeaux, often in blends (Saint Emilion, Pomerol, etc.), and the more restrained, considered wines from South Africa.

Nebbiolo

The infamous king of grapes in northwest Italy's Piedmont region, most easily found in Barolo and Barbaresco. Nebbiolo produces deceptively lightly coloured but enormously tannic, intensely aromatic wines. Cherry, rose petals and hot tar are the common, evocative tasting notes. The tannins will grip your cheeks firmly, whether it has been produced in either of the two common styles – vanilla-scented, lush, ripe, new-oak aged examples, or the more elegant, less-oak-dominated, varietally pure, long-aged wines. Never cheap, the best are many years mature. Have the protein-rich food ready to balance.

Further big reds to explore: Sangiovese, Tuscany; unfortified red blends of the Douro Valley; Rioja Reserva, Rioja; Primitivo, Puglia; and old-vine Garnacha blends in Priorat.

Sparkling Wine

The go-to celebratory style. I love sparkling for its ability to turn any occasion into a conscious moment of enjoyment. As a category, it remains hugely popular and is arguably becoming much more an 'everyday luxury' than it was a few decades ago. It's certainly helpful to know the key styles and to which situation each is best suited.

Traditional method wines, wherever they are grown, tend to have a more zingy acid structure, finer, more intense bubbles and more concentration of flavour. They are brilliant aperitifs but will stand up to a proper meal, too. The best pairings are those with crisp, fatty, salty elements to let the wine's acidity refresh the palate. The clean, citrus note in all the wines works a charm with every type of seafood. Charmat Method wines, like Prosecco, are softer structured and less concentrated, wherever they are grown, so are perfect with light dishes or as aperitifs.

Prosecco

Ubiquitous, a fizzy phenomenon. Often quite sweet, this is soft-textured, supremely easy-drinking, pear-scented bubbly. The best examples are from the smaller, DOCG-rated hillsides of Conegliano and Valdobbiadene, where the wines reach a remarkable finesse and intensity of flavour, compared to the average. 'Spumante' on the label means fully sparkling. Get to know 'frizzante' styles from the Veneto, too, which are much lighter sparkling, sometimes using the grape Glera and labelled as Prosecco, sometimes using the arguably more-exciting Garganega. Delicious, summery, light-lunch and aperitif wines.

Champagne

The benchmark. Over three hundred years of intentionally making sparkling wines in a cool climate. Chardonnay, Pinot Noir and Meunier (plus a rag-tag bunch of almost unused additional varieties) form the backbone of arguably the greatest sparkling wine of all time. The Grande Marques are great to take to parties and show your date how generous you are, but the really exciting exploration is in smaller grower–producers. Typically dry, relatively high acidity, with lemon and baked-orchard fruit characters and rich, fresh-bread aged notes. Try out different styles to get your bearings, too; NV blends, Blanc de Blancs, Blanc de Noirs, etc.

Cremant

The sparkling wines of France, outside the Champagne region. They often represent great value, as they are made in the same Traditional Method. Joyfully, they often use regionally distinct grape varieties, such as Chenin Blanc in Loire, Pinot Blanc and Gris in Alsace, and Mauzac in Limoux. Typically dry like Champagne, rarely do they achieve the same finesse and complexity as their famous counterpart, but they are exploratory and high quality.

English Sparkling

I may be biased, living locally and being intimately involved in the industry for over a decade, but England is almost inarguably the greatest place to make Traditional Method sparkling today. There may only be a very short history of commercial production – sixty years is stretching it a bit – but a wide spread of producers have gained international acclaim. The wines are Champagne-like, typically using the same key trio of grapes, but with a distinctive, fine, tart, citrus acidity and crisp, tree-fresh orchard fruit.

Cava

Oh, much-maligned Cava. The butt of so many jokes. Discount it at your peril, even the big brands make dry, refreshing, Traditional Method fizz at outrageously low prices, ideal for casual events and big-volume pouring. The best examples, including the entirely separate but important new Corpinnat category, are distinctly herbaceous, fuller-bodied, concentrated, elegant examples able to stand toe-to-toe with English sparkling and Champagne. Exciting indigenous grapes add intrigue and exploration.

Esoterica to explore further: Cap Classique, South Africa; Franciacorta and other Italian Traditional Method sparkling; Tasmanian sparkling wine; and Canadian sparkling wine.

Sweet Wine

Once the most revered and sought-after wines in the world, sales of sweet wine have been in steady decline for generations, mainly due to increasingly sugar-conscious societies and perhaps a reduction in the occasions that call for a properly sweet wine. Nevertheless, these are fantastic wines to serve with desserts, they play a great contrast to cheese courses and, frankly, can be a great alternative to a dessert full-stop. But, it's fair to say, even I, as a massive wine fan, only find an excuse to crack open a bottle and share it with friends a few times a year . . . I must try harder.

The best have a bold acidity to counter the high sugar levels. We are talking wines that can have up to 150g of sugar per litre here, some even more. For context cola is around 106g of sugar per litre. The combination of alcohol and sugar acts as a very good preservative, so they can be very long-lived.

Sauternes/Barsac

Southern Bordeaux regions producing some of the most sought-after and expensive sweet wines in the world. Botrytis (Noble Rot) is key here, caused by the distinct local climate, with morning mists influenced by the convergence of the nearby Garonne and Ciron rivers. Semillon and Sauvignon Blanc are key varieties. Age-worthy wines, the best of which can mature for decades, perhaps hundreds (!!) of years. Apricots, honey, ginger and baking spices are key notes to look out for.

Tokaji Aszú

Super-sweet, botrytis-affected wines made in northeast Hungary from local varieties Furmint and Hárslevelű, among others. Traditionally, baskets (puttony) of botrytis-shrivelled sweet grapes would have been added to a normal, non-botrytis grape juice, giving more sweetness with every basket added. These baskets became the labelling system to differentiate sweetness levels, a '6 Puttonyos' Tokaji is the sweetest Aszú style.

Beerenauslese (BA) and Trockenbeerenauslese (TBA) Riesling

Very sweet wines from Germany. Most commonly the Mosel Valley. Produced from a hundred per cent Riesling. Raisined on the vine by botrytis and picked by hand in multiple tranches through the steep vineyards very late in the harvest, BA is very sweet. TBA is picked even later and is even sweeter; in fact, one of the sweetest wines in the world. The prices can be steep, especially for the rare TBA. Acidity is key here; razor-sharp Riesling acidity keeps the wines very refreshing rather than syrupy and cloying. Clean apricot and dried fruits character with minerally, citrus zing.

Ice Wine

Produced in extremely cold climates from Canada to Germany. Grapes are left to freeze on the vine, as winter sets in. The frozen grapes are picked, pressed and the super-concentrated juice, high in sugar, acidity and flavours, is slowly fermented.

Ultra-sweet wines, only made in climates that consistently get cold enough to freeze the grapes. Germany requires it to be -7°C to produce Eiswein. Rare and very premium priced.

Recioto della Valpolicella

A sweet red wine made from (mostly) air-dried Corvina grapes. The same process as the dry, powerhouse red wine Amarone, but the grapes don't ferment fully, leaving a high quantity of residual sugars. Sweet red wines are fantastic with chocolate desserts. The drying concentrates the acidity, sugars and flavour, so expect intense cherry and red berry fruits.

Here are some further sweet wines to explore: Monbazillac, France; Malvasia Vin Liastos, Monemvasia, Greece; and Moscato d'Asti, Italy.

Fortified Wine

Another category of wine that we don't give enough time of day, fortified wines are some of the most exquisite, intensely flavoured, complex wines in the world. An amazing range of aromas and flavours are here to be found. You will find the most opulent wines, full of figs, dates, toasted nuts, nougat, burnt butter and chocolate. Then, others should be treated like a standard non-fortified wine. They are lean and dry and racy styles, incredible as an aperitif or with a bowl of olives. Across the board, fortified wines are some of the best-value, price-to-quality wines available in the UK.

The existence of most fortified wines harks back to the early days of international shipping. Wines were fortified to protect them on the long journey from the producer to the customer, often a journey lasting many months in warm conditions. For this reason, some fortified wines (Madeira is the main reference here) can age in the bottle literally forever, even after opening.

There are horses for courses, so the times to enjoy these wines are diverse. Lighter Fino and Manzanilla sherries are perfect early evening aperitifs. More intense styles of sherry and Ports are perfect cheeseboard pairers. Sweet fortifieds are great digestifs after dinner, or paired with a hefty dessert. Don't shy away from using fortified wines in cocktails either, there is a long history of their use. Fino and tonic and the Sherry Cobbler should be in everyone's repertoire.

Sherry

Based on Palomino Fino grapes grown around Jerez in southwest Spain's Andalucía. Flor-aged is a thick layer of yeast sediment that forms on the top of the Fino and Manzanilla wine, ageing in barrels in the bodegas. It protects the wine from oxidation. These dry wines, full of citrus, salinity and subtle nuttiness come under the Fino and Manzanilla style and sit at just 15 per cent ABV. Then, more boozy, mildly nutty, more complex Palo Cortado and Amontillado styles, followed by the rich, deeply savoury, nutty Oloroso form the 'sometimes dry, sometimes sweet and everything in between' sections. Extraordinary wines, aged in a unique solera system, fractionally blending barrels over many years to achieve complexity and un-matchable consistency of quality. Don't forget the low-priced, sweet cream, blended sherry styles. They're not cool, and are very grandma-chic, but they can be lots of fun.

Pedro Ximénez

Thick-skinned white grapes grown predominantly in Montilla-Moriles in Spain's Andalucía region. Making a sherry-type sweet wine and allowed as a component in sweet sherry blends. The grapes are picked, often with botrytis, and are dried in the sun to concentrate the sugars, acid and flavour. Fortified to cease fermentation and retain enormous sugar levels, these are dark in colour, thickly viscous, syrupy, lusciously sweet wines. Think raisins, figs, cocoa nibs and coffee bean aromas.

Madeira

Wines made on a tiny, foggy island in the Atlantic, an autonomous Portuguese region. A regular stop on the cross-Atlantic voyage between Europe and America, for centuries the island has produced some of the world's most unique fortified wines. Aged for long periods, often in the natural heat of the sun, barrels oxidise and the wine inside undergoes complex changes. The resulting wines are near indestructible, often with burnt butter *'rancio'* characters and nutty, caramelly delicious flavours. All have a piercing acidity, some are relatively dry, others very sweet. Try a ten-year-old Sercial (dry), a Boal or Malvasia (sweet), and perhaps a lower-price-point, ten-or-so-year-old blended Madeira to get into the groove.

Port (White, Tawny, Vintage)

The big name in fortified wines, surely? Produced in Portugal's Douro Valley, Port can be white, pink and red. Red is by far the most common. There are many styles, from easy-drinking, lower-price-point Ruby (a simple, fruity, boozy sipper), to the two main high-quality categories – Vintage (and the drink-it-now version Late Bottled Vintage) and Tawny. Vintage Ports are intense, long-aged in bottle and full of deep, intense black fruit flavours. They can age for decades. Tawny Ports are lighter in colour, long-aged in oak barrels and are for drinking on release. Nuttier, with layers of complex black and red fruits and herbal aroma. All styles have their place. Definitely for the cheese-board and the after-dinner digestif segment of the evening.

Rutherglen Muscat

Officially the sweetest wine in the world, regularly 250g of sugar per litre (a quarter of the liquid is sugar!) and sometimes over 300g of sugar per litre! Super-super-sweet, red muscat grapes, aged in barrel, often in hot tin sheds out in the heat of Rutherglen, a small region in Australia's Victoria. You can find them in merchants and some supermarkets. Definitely wines to drink with cheese or seriously sweet dessert. There is a hierarchy of increasingly old, increasingly sweet, increasingly expensive wines, I'd suggest starting with an opening price, always good 'Rutherglen', before investing in the next tier 'Classic'.

Other exotica to try: Marsala; and Moscatel de Setúbal.

Useful Resources

Berry Bros. & Rudd's website do great free-to-access vintage
reports for your assistance.
Wine Folly wine maps are unbeatable in their simplicity
and clarity.
Wine Grapes, J. Robinson, J. Harding and J. Vouillamoz
(London: Allen Lane, 2012)
Understanding Wine Technology, D. Bird and N. Quillé (London:
DBQA Publishing, 2021)
The Oxford Companion to Wine, (eds) J. Harding, J. Robinson
and T.Q. Thomas (Oxford: OUP, 2023)

Acknowledgements

Impossible without:

Matthew and Caroline Collins – Home from home. Family. Life-changing generosity. Love. Important to note, Matthew 'Taught me everything I know about wine'.

Clare Malec – From day one on a stage and every day since. Inspiring. Honest. Creative catalyst. Doer. Friend.

Olly Smith – Game changer. My break. Early doors hype-man. Harvey's Best. Friend.

Oz Clarke – The OG. Joie de vivre. Kindness. Respect. Inspiration. Shared vision. Friend.

Sancho Rocha – The spark. Most inspiring leader. Kind human. Great wine man.

Index

About the Author

A charismatic and engaging communicator, Tom has worked in the hospitality industry since he was fourteen. Aged twenty, he found himself at The Ivy in London, where a hero called Sancho taught him the basics of wine. Tom's route into the world of wine and his extraordinary experiences in the industry bring a rare, natural approach to the subject; full of love, warm wit and digestible wisdom, the antithesis to the staid, exclusive narrative that perseveres. A modern, relatable approach to wine.

Since The Ivy, wine has pulled Tom through roles building engaging wine-lists for restaurants, running international sales teams for industry-leading and up-and-coming wine producers, a bit of telly, a bit of radio, hundreds of live events and more. Right now, he tries, with moderate success, to balance his trade consultancy and media work alongside his young family.